need to know

Mushroom Hunting

Patrick Harding

Collins

First published in 2006 by Collins
an imprint of
HarperCollins Publishers
77–85 Fulham Palace Road
London W6 8JB

www.collins.co.uk

A catalogue record for this book is available from the British Library

Edited and designed by D & N Publishing

Editorial Director: Helen Brocklehurst
Editor: Emily Pitcher
Series design: Mark Thomson

Photographs © Patrick Harding except for the following: pp. 17 © HarperCollins; 24, 27b © Simon Booth/NHPA; 9, 45, 63t, 65, 67, 87, 89, 90, 95t, 99l, 132, 135, 143, 145t, 147, 150, 151l, 154, 155, 177t © Tony Lyon

p. 19 © Jean Binney

Front cover photograph: © Nigel Bean/Nature PL

Back cover photographs: © Patrick Harding

ISBN–13: 978-0-00-721507-X

Colour reproduction by Colourscan, Singapore
Printed and bound by Printing Express Ltd, Hong Kong

Contents

Introduction: what is a mushroom?

For thousands of years, living things were divided into just two separate kingdoms: plants and animals. Fungi, the scientific term for the group of organisms that includes edible mushrooms, were placed in the plant kingdom.

Plants like this foxglove are autotrophic – they make their own food (initially sugars) using sunlight as an energy source. Plants are composed of cells that have rigid walls made of cellulose.

Like plants, fungi are 'rooted' in places and they reproduce by spores that are comparable to those produced by ferns and mosses. Because fungi lack leaves (and so, unlike green plants, cannot manufacture carbohydrates using energy from sunlight), they were considered to be unusual plants.

Around 300 years ago it was proposed that, as fungi differed considerably from plants and animals, they should be placed in their own kingdom. However, it was not until the latter part of the 20th century that scientists fully embraced the idea of a separate fungal kingdom. Much of the media and general public still consider mushrooms to be plants, and mycologists (people who study fungi) mostly work in botanical gardens, university botany departments, or with forestry or agricultural institutes – hence the plant link remains.

must know

Animals are heterotrophic which means that they require a food source, which they ingest and digest internally. Animal cells lack the rigid wall that plant cells have.

Fungi are also heterotrophic, but they digest and absorb their nutrients from external food sources, through tube-like threads called hyphae.

Within the fungal kingdom are thousands of visually insignificant species known as the microfungi. These include moulds, mildews and rusts. In contrast, the macrofungi produce their spores in a complex fruit body that is readily visible to the naked eye. A mushroom is a macrofungus whose large fruit body is collected and eaten.

'Mushroom' is a word with at least three different meanings. As used in the title of the Collins Gem Guide to *Mushrooms*, it embraces the macrofungi, including edible, inedible and poisonous species. The term mushroom is also used to refer solely to edible species such as the Parasol Mushroom, the remaining non-edible species (especially the poisonous ones) being called toadstools (*see* page 180). Finally, mycologists reserve the word mushroom for a limited number of species such as the Field Mushroom and the Cultivated Mushroom, which belong to a small group of fungi in the genus *Agaricus* (*see* page

Branched Oyster Mushrooms ready for cleaning and cooking.

Agaricus campestris – **the edible and well-known Field Mushroom.**

80). As we shall see, some species of *Agaricus* are mildly toxic; to the mycologist these are poisonous mushrooms! In this book it is assumed that mushroom hunters will be looking for edible species (not all of which are in the genus *Agaricus*) but will also encounter other fungi. This is why the book includes a final section on poisonous species.

1 Getting started

You don't need to be a scientist to be interested in mushrooms. More importantly, it isn't necessary to drive into the countryside to find them – gardens, parks and playing fields all play host to a wide range of fungus species. For those intending to consume some of their finds, caution is the watchword, summed up in the saying: 'There are lots of bold mushroom hunters, but not many old, bold mushroom hunters'.

Taking the first steps

In many countries such as France, Italy and Poland, mushroom hunting has long been a popular hobby and, for some people, also an important source of income.

Innovative mushroom hunters using a hat to collect St George's Mushrooms.

Exactly why the British have a history of distaste for wild fungi in marked contrast to most of our European neighbours, is open to debate. The Pilgrim Fathers exported our distrust of fungi to America, where historically there has been a similar reluctance towards mushroom hunting.

An increased interest in mushroom hunting in Britain was initiated by the food shortages during and after World War II, when a number of booklets (including one published by the government) promoted the collection of wild mushrooms. At the same time, the integration of many Polish men who had fought alongside British troops in the war introduced people from a culture with a long history of using wild mushrooms as food. They must have been pleasantly surprised to find so little competition from the British!

In the late 1950s and through the 1960s, as Britain shook off the shortages of the immediate post-war days, the middle classes began to venture across the Channel for their holidays. There they found cheap wine and novel foods. In the French markets and Italian restaurants the British discovered that mushrooms were not restricted to the one or two species, as in the greengrocers back home.

British delicatessens began to increase their stock of tinned truffles and dried Ceps, but the general phobia surrounding the eating of self-collected wild mushrooms (with the exception of

Field and Horse mushrooms) continued. One good reason for this, even as late as the 1970s, was the lack of good mushroom identification books aimed at the general public.

All this began to change in the 1980s, with the publication of a number of guides to identifying fungi (*see* page 189) and the rise in popularity of the mushroom-loving Italian chef Antonio Carluccio. Even then, despite increased coverage on television, mushroom hunting was still very much a minority sport. During the 1990s, however, restaurateurs discovered the pulling power of 'wild' mushroom dishes and commercial collecting became viable. At the same time, the choice of shop-bought species increased enormously and a number of books concentrating solely on the edible wild species were published.

Fortunately, attitudes have changed and more British people are now enjoying the delights of foraging for fungi as a source of free food.

A mushroom market stall in Brussels in 1984.

What kind of mushroom hunter are you?

The public's increased fascination with mushrooms and toadstools is not confined to just those people with a culinary interest. For hundreds of years, mushrooms were associated with the Devil and the Antichrist. This view suppressed scientific work on fungi, and their classification as plants did little to help the situation.

Scientists had already discovered that fungi formed close relationships with trees, but it was not until towards the end of the 20th century that they began to realise that non-woody flowering plants, ferns and mosses also form close associations with fungi.

The presence of certain species of fungi is increasingly being used as an indicator of undisturbed habitats and potential Sites of Special Scientific Interest (SSSIs). This evidence can be collected only by people who can accurately identify the many different species of mushroom and toadstool, so mycologists (including amateurs) are in demand!

The rare Oak Polypore (*Piptoporus quercinus*) grows on ancient Oak trees and is a valuable indicator of former deer parks and other important long-term habitats.

Wooden mushrooms as garden ornaments.

Amateur mushroom hunters include those with a general interest in natural history, especially wild flowers, as well as those who seek a new challenge. Many entomologists (people who study insects) have become expert at the identification of certain fungi that serve as food for the developing larvae of flies and other insects.

Mushrooms and toadstools have become important images in the arts and crafts movement, and the popularity of garden ornamental mushrooms, turned wooden toadstools and pottery fungi has soared. As a result, people attending mushroom courses are as likely to be potters or painters as they are to be naturalists or gourmet cooks. The fantastic range of shapes, colours and textures exhibited by fungi make wonderful subjects for artists, and mushrooms and toadstools are treated as honorary plants by the growing band of botanical artists (*see* page 19). My own interest in mushrooms first developed as I attempted to put names to the photographs I had taken of them.

There are also thousands of mushroom hunters who ignore Field Mushrooms and other edible species, searching only for the hallucinogenic Magic Mushroom (*see* page 70). Whether people enjoy mushroom hunting for scientific, aesthetic, culinary or more way-out reasons, the hobby is increasing in popularity all the time.

Fungi through the year

The British public's lack of knowledge about the fungal kingdom is not helped by the timing of television shows, radio programmes and newspaper articles on edible wild mushrooms.

With very few exceptions, these appear in September and October. In addition, the events calendar of many local natural history societies includes an annual fungal foray (an excursion to look for fungi) during September or October. The general impression is that autumn is the only active season for the mushroom hunter.

If the same limited approach was applied to wild flowers, with excursions restricted to June and July, botanists would be too late for the flowering of such species as Lesser Celandine and too early for autumn species like Marsh Gentian. Older books about fungi, while acknowledging that a few edible species fruit during spring and early summer, assume that most of the rest are restricted to the autumn. However, since 1970, records of fungi collected throughout the year have provided more accurate information about their fruiting seasons.

must know

Given our changing climate (especially our milder winters), many autumn-fruiting fungi are now continuing well into the winter and some summer-fruiting species are starting growth as early as April.

Expert guidance being offered on an annual fungal foray.

Spring: March, April and May

Early spring is often associated with cold, damp soils, but as temperatures rise so conditions become more favourable for the production of fungal fruit bodies. After the winter, grass swards are shorter, many of the trees are devoid of leaves and there is only limited ground cover in woodlands, so early season mushrooms are easier to spot.

Some of the best edible species are restricted to springtime. The short season for morels (*see* page 126) can start as early as March in southern England and rarely continues after the end of May, even in the north of the country. In any locality, morel fruiting dates tend to be consistent from year to year. St George's Mushrooms (*see* page 102) start to appear in March and numbers usually peak during May.

Edible species with winter-fruiting seasons extending into the spring include the Velvet Shank (*see* page 160) and Oyster Mushroom (*see* page 164). In May, some grassland species such as the Fairy Ring Champignon (*see* page 104) and Giant Puffball (*see* page 108) put in their first appearances. With the exception of the False Morel (*see* page 129), very few poisonous species fruit before the summer – an added bonus for the early mushroom hunter.

An April feast of morels and St George's Mushrooms.

good to know

As with the first dates for frog spawn, returning Swallows and the flowering of Bluebells, there is a general progression for the dates of fungal fruiting, with the earliest spring records in the south. For autumn records, however, the generally wetter parts of Scotland and Wales are often ahead of the south and east, especially in those years with a dry summer.

Summer: June, July and August

For the mushroom hunter seeking grassland fungi, June is often a fruitful time, although July and August are frequently too dry. This is less of a problem for species that obtain their water from living or dead wood, or directly from tree roots, and by August some of the woodland fungi start to appear.

Summer is the best time for finding fresh Giant Puffballs (*see* page 108), while other early grassland fungi include Field and Horse mushrooms (*see* pages 85 and 87) and Lawyer's Wig (*see* page 94), all of which reach their peak in autumn. Fresh edible brackets of Chicken of the Woods (*see* page 170) are most frequent in summer, as is the Branched Oyster Mushroom (*see* page 165). Other early fruiting woodland species include the Deceiver (*see* page 148), Charcoal Burner (*see* page 137), Yellow Swamp Russula (*see* page 139), Chanterelle (*see* page 130), and Bay and Birch boletes (*see* pages 118 and 121).

Autumn: September, October and November

This is the most fruitful season, especially for grassland edibles. However, September can be poor in dry years and early frost or snow may bring an abrupt end to the fruiting of most fungal species. Grassland fungi that are most abundant in autumn include various species of mushroom and others mentioned in the summer section, with the addition of the Meadow Wax Cap

The grassland wax caps are mostly autumn-fruiting fungi.

(*see* page 106), parasol mushrooms (*see* page 98), Field Blewit (*see* page 96) and the smaller puffballs (*see* page 110).

Of the woodland edibles, Beefsteak Fungus (*see* page 168), Hen of the Woods (*see* page 172) and Wood Cauliflower (*see* page 174) are all autumn species. This is the time when Horn of Plenty (*see* page 134) and various edible boletes, russulas and milk caps are most abundant, if partially obscured by fallen leaves, while buried in the soil is Summer Truffle (*see* page 177). Honey Fungus (*see* page 156) and Wood Blewit (*see* page 97) often delay fruiting until October, but they frequently carry on into the winter season.

Winter: December, January and February

A number of grassland species continue fruiting into December in mild winters. These include the Meadow Wax Cap (*see* page 106), Field Blewit (*see* page 96) and Lawyer's Wig (*see* page 94). Woodland species are less affected by light frosts, and the Saffron Milk Cap (*see* page 140), Chanterelle (*see* page 130), Honey Fungus (*see* page 156) and some of the boletes all fruit into December in small numbers. Wood Blewit (*see* page 97) continues through to February, while the Oyster Mushroom (*see* page 164) and Velvet Shank (*see* page 160) are in their element during the winter. And don't forget Jew's Ear (*see* page 162), which fruits year-round!

Photographing and illustrating fungi

Being able to record fungal finds as photographs or illustrations is not only important if rare species require verification, but it also provides a personalised reference to help with future identification problems. As a bonus, good images of mushrooms and toadstools make excellent art.

did you know?

Surprisingly good pictures of fungi can be obtained by placing them on a flat-bed scanner.

Until the start of the 21st century, the preferred choice for the fungal photographer was an SLR (single lens reflex) camera using 35mm print or transparency film and fitted with a macro close-up lens. Such a system enables the production of life-size, or larger-than-life, images.

Unlike other natural history subjects such as birds (and even flowers that sway in the wind), fungi don't usually move while being filmed, but as many are woodland species the main problem is a lack of light. The wide lens aperture required under low light conditions gives a very small depth of field (the area in sharp focus) and can result in blurred pictures. The most obvious way round this is to use a flash, but this is not easy with very close-up work and it can result in an unnatural, blacked-out background.

Taking your photographs lying down will eliminate camera shake and ensure an interesting view of the old puffballs.

Instead, a mini tripod (or spike driven into the ground) used as a camera rest enables a long exposure time (more light is let in) without camera shake.

The easiest solution to the light problem is to use a fast film. For all but the darkest subjects this can negate the need for a flash or tripod. The huge improvement in film technology has meant that poster-size prints can now be made from images on 400 ASA film without the grainy image previously associated with fast film.

The availability of high-resolution digital cameras at a reasonable price has provided a realistic alternative to film cameras for the fungal photographer. The slow reaction time associated with digital photography is not a problem with most fungal subjects. The model of digital camera suitable for taking shots of scenery and people will not, however, necessarily be suitable for close-up pictures of toadstools.

It is important to buy a digital camera with a high pixel (picture element) number, preferably at least 4 million. You will need a macro mode for close-up shots, but be aware that with digital cameras there are two systems of zoom, enabling close-up and magnified images. Optical zoom, using the camera lens, is far superior to digital zoom in terms of the quality of the resulting

Digital cameras are now a popular choice. Ensure you choose one with a high pixel number for best results.

want to know more?

For an overview of buying and using a digital camera, see *Digital Photography* by Patrick Hook, in the Collins Need to Know? series.

must know

Many fungi are taller than they are wide, and thus are best photographed in portrait rather than landscape format.

images. High-resolution images require a lot of memory, so you will also need to buy a large memory card.

Regardless of the type of camera you have, there are some key points to remember when photographing fungi for identification purposes. First, the habitat of a fungus is an important clue to its identification, as is the substrate on which it is growing. If a toadstool is growing on a tree stump, include part of the stump in the picture. Remember that colour and surface texture may change after collection, so try to photograph fungi in the field rather than back at home.

By far the most common mistake is to photograph a mushroom only from above. If a photograph does not show the colour and shape of the gills or pores, or such important stem features as a ring or basal volva (*see* page 39), it will be worthless as an identification aid. If possible, include a range of specimens at different developmental stages, with at least one showing the cap underside and stem details. The size of a fruit body can be difficult to determine from a photograph, so it is worth

An attractive shot of Velvet Foot, but it doesn't show the velvety stem!

including either a coin or natural object, such as a pine cone, as a scale.

For fungi photographed after collection, it is worth including the spore print where taken (*see* page 39) with the specimen – this provides an important clue as to the identification of the fungus. Sometimes, the most arty-looking shots are the least useful in ascertaining identification – a feature to be remembered when buying identification books.

In addition to the written records you keep, it is often worthwhile including visual representations – either photographs or your own artwork. Using an unlined notebook allows you to include pencil or ink field sketches. Watercolours may cause the buckling of thin notebook paper, so you may prefer to paint at home on either hot-pressed or cold-pressed (also called 'not') 140lb watercolour paper. These paintings may then be inserted into a notebook in the same way as a photographic print. In any case, the time required to execute a full watercolour painting normally precludes such work from being done in the field.

Where possible, illustrate subjects at life size and colour match carefully. Close observation is as important as artistic talent. The inclusion of several individuals at different angles will illustrate a fuller range of features. Note also that specimens placed fresh in a fridge for artwork reference must be kept upright, as the angle between the cap and stem on a fungus left on its side will alter, rather like a sitter moving during a portrait painting.

Books with good watercolour illustrations include *The Young Specialist Looks at Fungi* by Hans Haas (1969) and *Les Champignons* (Beatrix Potter, 1996).

Watercolour of Magic Mushrooms.

Equipment

Unlike many other hobbies, mushroom hunting does not require any expensive purchases at the outset. Given the importance of water for the growth of mushrooms, a good pair of stout, waterproof shoes or walking boots is a must-have, together with warm, waterproof clothing.

Jeans are not a good idea, as constant kneeling on wet grass or soil can make for uncomfortable conditions. An anorak pocket large enough to carry this book will limit the unnecessary collection of non-edibles. Remember that a final identification of the collection needs to be done back at home; spore prints (*see* page 39) can't be made in the field.

The most important item to the mushroom hunter is the collecting basket. Plastic bags are to be avoided because their contents tend to heat up and sweat, so hastening their decay. Also, the temptation with carrier bags is to keep piling more mushrooms in on top, thus crushing those near the bottom. After a long foray, the contents of a plastic bag can resemble mushroom soup – one that could include a dangerous mix of edible and poisonous species.

The parcel shelf of a hatchback makes a good place to display the day's finds.

There is a certain amount of snobbery concerning collecting baskets. All that is required is a lightweight shallow carrier that is easily held in one hand (or, better still, on an arm, keeping both hands free for making notes). An open-weave willow basket is ideal, as it ensures good air circulation, although wooden trugs are lighter and shallower than most willow baskets. Cheaper still are the free cardboard (or plastic) mushroom punnets sometimes available from fruit shops. Some form of cover to keep out the rain is an optional extra.

A penknife (or a special mushroom knife with a brush at the handle end) is essential for the careful removal of intact mushrooms from soil or wood. That said, there is no scientific evidence that cutting the stem does less harm to the mycelium (*see* page 26) than teasing out the whole fruit body (twist and pull, as with rhubarb). The latter method is actually far safer for the beginner – cutting the stem and leaving a partially buried volva behind (*see* page 39) makes identification of the many poisonous *Amanita* species much more difficult. Cut (or brush) away any dirt from the stem base and check for maggots before adding finds to your basket. Keep your knife fastened on a chain connected to your belt to save losing it.

must know

To protect more delicate species and to help keep edible and poisonous species apart, purchase some small paper bags from a local food shop and number them. Place each species in a separate numbered bag once you have made field notes about it in your pocket notebook or electronic equivalent. You can then easily separate the species for any more detailed identification checks later on. However, don't leave the fungi in this unventilated state for too long.

A high-power microscope.

A walking or thumb stick to clear away bracken and other vegetation in the search for fungi is a good idea only if you need support; otherwise it takes up another hand and is something else to lose. More useful when it comes to checking fine details, such as how the gills are attached, is a hand lens giving ×10 magnification Special mushroom-cleaning brushes are also available, although a toothbrush does the job just as well.

For the mushroom hunter solely interested in collecting edible species, the only other equipment needed is a means to dry and preserve the fungi (*see* page 59). Those wishing to identify all fungal finds will soon realise that the separation of some species is not possible on the basis of the macroscopic features used in this book. At this stage, the main expense is the purchase of a high-power microscope. This will allow the size, shape and ornamentation of the spores to be determined, as well as the alignment of hyphae (*see* page 26) in thin slices of cap flesh. Such features are diagnostic in the separation of similar-looking species. At this stage, the hobby can become an obsession – beware!

Sources of information

Given that there are more than 6,000 different species of larger fungi in the British Isles, the first requirement for a mushroom hunter is a reliable identification book. Prior to 1980, the number of mushroom identification books aimed at the general public could be counted on the fingers of one hand, and most of them were translations of books previously published in mainland Europe. However there are now several on the market.

When choosing a field guide, take a careful look at the pictures. Photographs of fungi need to be sharp and must show both upper and lower surfaces, preferably also including more than one specimen. Good watercolour illustrations may contain more detail than can be provided in a single photograph. The printing quality is also important. Many people like to have more than one book, so that they have both photographs and illustrations with which to compare their finds. *See* Need to Know More?, page 189 for some recommendations.

want to know more?

Many organisations run single-day, weekly or residential courses on the identification of mushrooms and toadstools, some with an emphasis on edibles. These include local adult education classes, run by universities, Workers' Educational Associations (WEAs) and the like. Useful contacts are:
- ▶ the National Trust (www.nationaltrust.org.uk/events);
- ▶ the Field Studies Council (www.field-studies-council.org);
- ▶ Madingley Hall, Cambridge (www.cont-ed.cam.ac.uk);
- ▶ Urchfont Manor, Wiltshire (email: urchfontmanor@wiltshire.gov.uk);
- ▶ Plas Tan y Bwlch, Snowdonia (www.plastanybwlch.com).
- ▶ Keep a mushroom diary. This records not only the exact location of finds for future reference, but also the dates of finds.
- ▶ Two excellent suppliers of mushroom-hunting equipment, identification books and growing kits have websites at www.mycologue.co.uk and www.jac-by-the-stowl.co.uk.

A group of happy mushroom hunters taking part in a residential course.

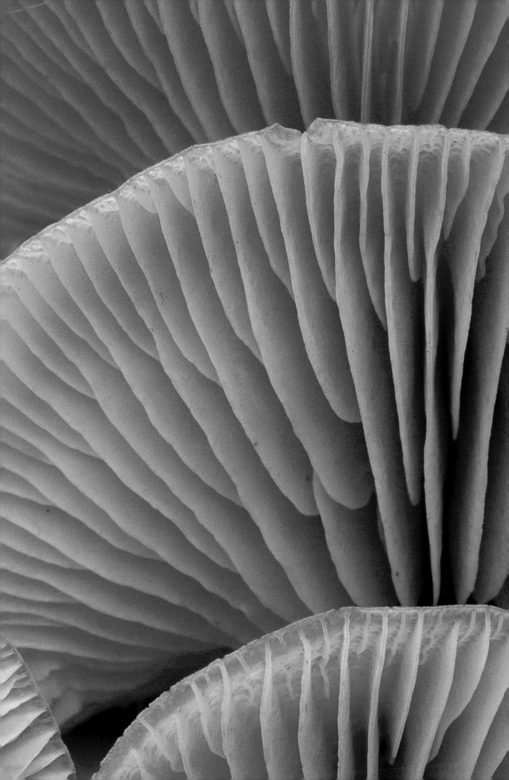

2 About fungi

In order to be able to locate and identify mushrooms and toadstools accurately, it is necessary to know something about their lifestyle, the way they are split into groups and what features to look out for. Many fungi are restricted to a particular habitat, information that is useful in both finding and identifying species.

What are fungi and what do they do?

The fungal kingdom consists of a group of organisms that differ widely in their complexity, size, shape, colour and means of reproduction.

At one end of the spectrum are microfungi, such as the simple yeasts used for making bread and alcohol, and the moulds, some of which spoil our food while others provide us with valuable antibiotics. At the other end are species of macrofungi, including those with bracket-shaped fruit bodies up to a metre across, as well as the more familiar mushrooms and toadstools.

In marked contrast to the multicellular nature of most animals and plants, the majority of fungi are built up of long, thin, tubular filaments known as hyphae. A single hypha is like a minute, thin-walled drinking straw some five to twenty thousandths of a millimetre in diameter (about a tenth the diameter of a human hair), and can only be observed using a high-power microscope. In the macrofungi, the hyphae contain a fluid-based living material and are divided into segments by cross-walls. As in plant and animal cells, these segments contain hereditary material.

When supplied with food and moisture, fungal hyphae grow and branch from their tips. Growth rates in excess of 5mm an hour have been recorded, helping to explain the rapid size increase observed in many moulds. The mass of branching hyphae is known as a mycelium, and this is usually clearly visible to the naked eye as a cobweb-like collection of strands in soil, leaf litter or rotting wood. The general term

A microfungus whose hyphae are feeding on bread.

must know

Fungi are built of long tiny tubes called hyphae. The mass of branching hyphae is called a mycelium.

'spawn' is used to refer to the mycelium of mushrooms cultivated for their culinary or hallucinogenic properties.

The mycelium of an individual fungus may extend over a very wide area. In some toadstools it spreads as an expanding disc in the soil, and its size is revealed only by the above-ground ring of fruit bodies that are produced near the periphery of the mycelium (*see* the Fairy Ring pictured below). Mycelial growth enables an individual fungus to reach new food sources. Using DNA analysis, American mycologists have found evidence for the mycelial spread of an individual Honey Fungus extending over 15 hectares, with a calculated age in excess of 1,500 years. It seems that some fungi are among the largest and most long-lived organisms on Earth.

Mycelial threads of an ink cap (*Coprinus* sp.) among leaf litter.

A ring of fruit bodies, indicating the extent of the fungus's underground mycelium.

The heartwood of this Elm tree has been reduced to sawdust by lignin-digesting fungi.

Fungal hyphae absorb nutrients by breaking down plant (and animal) tissues, thus bringing about decay.

A leaf, in which the softer tissue has been digested by fungi.

Fungal hyphae spread over and penetrate potential food sources, from which they absorb water and small molecules, including glucose. Unlike plants, fungi cannot make their own food, and in a manner comparable to the digestive tract of higher animals, fungal hyphae produce a range of enzymes that break down complex substances into smaller, more readily absorbed compounds. Enzymes that degrade cellulose (found in plant cell walls) are present in fungal species that feed on plant material, including dead leaves. Some species produce enzymes that break down lignin, a chemical compound forming cell walls which is found in the woody trunks and branches of trees. Fungi are often restricted to certain habitats (*see* pages 40–53) and substrates by nature of their constituent enzymes.

Many fungi are saprophytic which means they live on dead plant (or animal) remains. There are even some fungi that live on the remains of other fungi. Others are parasitic and obtain their food from living organisms, which they may kill in the process, and some fungi form symbiotic relationships with other organisms to the benefit of both. Fungi help bring about decay and the recycling of nutrients, both essential processes for life on our planet.

The mycelium of a fungus represents its vegetative stage. Only a few species of fungi can be identified from the visual appearance of their mycelium, and in any case most mycelia are hidden from view within the soil, tree trunk or other substrate that is their food. Some fungi may remain in the mycelial stage for many years, spreading and propagating by fragmentation of the mycelium.

Sexual propagation of fungi is by spores – tiny, mostly single-celled bodies similar to those found in ferns and mosses, and produced by hyphae in special fruit bodies. This is the norm for macrofungi (including mushrooms and toadstools), but many fungi rarely, if ever, produce sexual spores. The hyphae in a fruit body are much more densely packed than those in a vegetative mycelium.

The production of fruit bodies brings fungi to our attention, and their features are widely used for classification and identification. The major groups of fungi, based on their fruit body (and spore) type, are described on pages 30–33.

The environmental and physiological triggers that initiate the formation of a young fruit body (primordium), and the subsequent expansion of the tiny but fully formed fruit body, are not the same for all species (*see* pages 12–15). The availability of moisture and minimum temperature levels are just two factors frequently involved.

A common lichen (*Cladonia* sp.) with fungus-like fruit bodies. A lichen is a symbiotic relationship between a fungus and an alga.

What different sorts of fungi are there?

Carl Linnaeus, the 18th-century Swedish naturalist who helped to standardise the naming and classification of plants and animals, lumped all the fungi together under a category he called 'Chaos'.

Since that time, taxonomy of the larger fungi (those of interest to the edible-mushroom hunter) has been refined, although confusion has not been totally banished.

Under modern schemes of fungal classification, one phylum (main group) is called the Basidiomycota, members of which produce sexual spores on a club-shaped structure termed a basidium. The group includes cereal rusts, other plant parasites, and most of the mushrooms and toadstools. The latter two belong to the class (subgroup) Basidiomycetes, of which there are more than 3,000 species native to Britain.

In contrast to members of the Basidiomycota phylum, there is a huge group of fungi that produce their sexual spores inside an elongated hyphal segment called an ascus. The Ascomycota, or Ascomycetes as they are more commonly known, include many microscopic fungi, moulds and yeasts. Of about 5,500 British species so far described, more than 1,800 form a symbiotic relationship with another organism (usually an alga) and are better known as lichens.

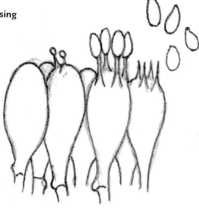

Basidia releasing their spores.

Basidiomycete fungi

Scientists disagree over the number, nature and naming of categories within the Basidiomycetes, but amateur mushroom hunters need only be able to recognise seven types, of which the first contains nearly all the familiar edible species.

1. **Parrot Wax Cap (***Hygrocybe psittacina***) grows on lawns and unimproved pasture land.**

1. **Agarics**. With mushroom-shaped fruit bodies bearing gills or tubes under the cap. The fruit bodies are soft and usually short-lived. There are about 2,200 species in Britain, including many of the edible species described in this book.

2. **Wood Hedgehog (***Hydnum repandum***), showing the spine-like projections under the cap.**

2. **Hedgehog fungi**. With spines under the cap. Most are short-lived and relatively soft-textured. There are only about 20 species in Britain, but these include several excellent edible species (*see* page 132).

3. **Stomach fungi**. These include the bag-like puffballs and earthballs, which are firm-fleshed when young but may later persist for months in a dry, leathery state. There are more than 100 species in Britain, many of which are edible when young (*see* pages 110 and 114).

3. **Mosaic Puffball (***Calvatia utriformis***), including the remains of an old fruit body.**

4. **Club and coral fungi**. These include the fairy clubs and number about 100 species in Britain. They are small, beautiful fungi that are of aesthetic rather than culinary interest. Some authorities consider that the larger, edible Wood Cauliflower (*see* page 174) is closely related to this group.

4. **The tiny White Spindles (***Clavaria vermicularis***) growing in short grass.**

5. Wrinkle-like folds on the underside of Chanterelle (*Cantharellus cibarius*).

6. Many-zoned Polypore (*Coriolus versicolor*), a common bracket fungus that grows on dead wood.

7. Orange Jelly Fungus (*Dacrymyces stillatus*) festooning a dead branch.

5. **Chanterelles and relatives**. This is an intermediate group, with the agaric shape but lacking true gills (*see* page 130 for details of the edible species).

6. **Bracket fungi** (often known as the polypores). These are shelf-like wood-rotters that grow on living trees or dead wood. Most have hard, long-lasting fruit bodies with tiny tubes on the underside. There are about 100 species in Britain, of which only a few (those with softer fruit bodies) are edible (*see* pages 168–173). There are also more than 300 inedible corticioid fungus species, which form pancake-like patches on logs and branches.

7. **Jelly fungi**. This is a rather unnatural group, in which many of the larger members produce fruit bodies that have a strangely gelatinous texture. Some, such as the Yellow Brain Fungus, are parasitic on corticioid fungi, while others, including the edible Jew's Ear (*see* page 162) and cultivated Wood-ear, grow on dead wood. The group includes more than 200 British species, including many microscopic ones.

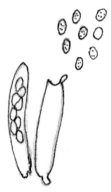

Asci releasing their spores.

Ascomycete fungi

Aside from the microscopic fungi, moulds, yeast and lichen fungi classed as Ascomycetes, the remainder of species in the group are placed in two subgroups based on the shape and structure of their fruit body.

1. **Cup fungi** (also known as the Discomycetes). Many of these live on dead vegetation and produce minute, soft, disc-shaped fruit bodies about 1mm in diameter. Larger, edible species include Orange Peel Fungus (*see* page 152). More complex shapes are found in the saddle fungi and the brain-like, edible morels (*see* pages 126–129). The highly prized subterranean enclosed fruit bodies of the truffles (*see* page 176) also belong to this group.

2. **Flask fungi** (also known as Pyrenomycetes). Most of these species produce tiny flask-shaped fruit bodies that are often hidden in plant tissue. A few produce much larger, hard, burnt-looking structures in which the fruit bodies are set, including Candle-snuff Fungus (*Xylaria hypoxylon*), Dead Man's Fingers (*X. polymorpha*) and King Alfred's Cakes (*Daldinia concentrica*). Despite the name of the latter, all three of these are hard and inedible.

1. The cup-like fruit body of a species of *Peziza* growing on damp soil.

2. The tough, tiny fruit body of Candle-snuff Fungus (*Xylaria hypoxylon*) growing on a tree stump.

Scientific names

Taxonomists pigeon-hole living organisms into taxa (groups), and also attempt to determine the hierarchical relationship between the different taxa.

want to know more?

In 2003, a list of recommended standard common English names for 1,000 species of fungi was published by the British Mycological Society. However, many of these differed from those already in use, and unfortunately the list has never met with universal approval from mycologists. The list can be downloaded from the society's website at www.britmycolsoc.org.

Once this has been done for a species (and it has been described in print), it is given a scientific (Latin) name. This name is generally written in italics and consists of two words – the first, with an initial capital letter, is the genus name, while the second, all in lower case, is the specific epithet. A genus is a taxon of closely related species, all of which share the same first word of their scientific name. Using Shaggy Ink Cap (*Coprinus comatus*) as an example, *Coprinus* is the genus name and *comatus* the specific epithet. The Common Ink Cap (*Coprinus atramentarius*) shares many features with the Shaggy Ink Cap (*see* pages 94–95) and so is placed in the same genus and shares the same first word of its scientific name.

good to know

Many black-spored agarics with non-dissolving gills are placed in the genus *Psathyrella*, which are then pulled together with other black-spored genera such as *Coprinus* in the family Coprinaceae. Other families that share features with Coprinaceae are put together with it in the order Agaricales. The remaining agarics are classified into two other orders: the Boletales, which include tube-bearing species such as the Cep (*see* page 116); and the Russulales, woodland species with a very brittle texture, such as the Saffron Milk Cap (*see* page 140).

KINGDOM	FUNGI
PHYLUM	BASIDIOMYCOTA
CLASS	BASIDIOMYCETES
SUB-CLASS	AGARICS
ORDER	AGRICALES
FAMILY	COPRINACEAE
GENUS	COPRINUS
SPECIES	COMATUS

Identifying fungi

When attempting to identify a bird, its overall size and colour are rarely sufficient alone, so details such as behaviour, song, beak shape and colour are all used as valuable additional clues.

Mushroom hunters don't have to learn about behaviour or song, but, as with birds, overall colour and size are not particularly useful when trying to recognise fungi. Because mushrooms don't fly, it is easy to take specimens home for identification, although the wise mushroom hunter makes a note of the important features of a fungus *before* putting it in the collecting basket.

Two of the most useful features that are critical for the accurate identification of mushrooms are habitat and substrate (where and on what they are growing). For example, some species are restricted to short grassland, disturbed ground or Beech woodland on chalk (*see* pages 40–53).

Check to see if the mushroom is growing on bare soil, moss, leaf litter or a living tree, or if there is a hidden tree stump or cow pat at its base. For fungi found on wood or in woodland, tree identification (which is essential) may require the collection of twig and leaf samples and the use of a guide to trees. Be aware that 'woodland' fungi can

Saffron Milk Cap (*Lactarius deliciosus*) growing under pine – note the needles on the cap.

occur in gardens, by hedges and within the root spread of a tree, which may be as far as 25m into a meadow.

The majority of edible fungi produce soft, ephemeral fruit bodies with an umbrella-like cap and stem. Most of the agarics, as the mushroom-shaped species are called, have thin vertical gills radiating beneath the cap in a pattern like that of bicycle spokes. In Ceps and other boletes (*see* pages 116–125), a mass of vertical tubes replaces the gills, while the Wood Hedgehog (*see* page 132) has downward-pointing spines instead of gills.

Key features of agaric fruit bodies

The descriptions in this book make minimum use of scientific terms for ease of understanding, but failure on the part of the edible-mushroom hunter to recognise a range of key features can make the difference between sickness and health.

Bell-shaped caps.

Cap showing red coloration after handling.

Cap
Size
▶ What is the cap diameter in centimetres of a mature specimen?
Shape
▶ Is the cap conical, bell-shaped, convex, flattened, depressed or funnel-shaped?
▶ Is the cap any of the above shapes and with a central hump?
▶ Is the cap margin inrolled, wavy, split or grooved?
Colour
▶ Is the cap colour uniform, or are there areas of a different colour?

- ▶ Is the central area of the cap darker or lighter?
- ▶ Is the cap paler near the margin as it dries out?
- ▶ Does the cap colour change on handling (bruising)?

Texture
- ▶ Is the cap smooth or wrinkled, dry or moist, glutinous (sticky) or mealy (covered with tiny particles)?
- ▶ Does the cap have darker fibres, scales or remnants ('spots') of the sheet-like universal veil (as seen in the poisonous *Amanita* group)?

Caps covered with darker scales.

Gills
Protection
- ▶ Are the immature gills/pores of young specimens hidden by a sheet or cobweb-like partial veil?

Cobweb-like veil covering immature gills.

Attachment
- ▶ Are the gills free (not attached to the stem), sinuate (narrowing abruptly near the stem), adnexed (narrowly attached), adnate (fully attached) or decurrent (running down onto the stem)?

Spacing
- ▶ Are intermediate gills present towards the cap margin?
- ▶ Are the gills distant (well spaced) or crowded (close together)?

Sinuate gills.

Texture
- ▶ Are the gills thin, thick, brittle, waxy or deliquescent (dissolving into a black fluid), or do they bleed a watery or milky latex when damaged?

Crowded gills (*left*) and distant gills with short intermediate gills (*right*).

Decurrent gills exuding a milky latex when scratched.

Black gills.

Large, angular, orange-red pores.

Gills (cont)

Colour

▶ Check a range of gill stages – in older mushrooms spore colour may mask the gill colour. Look for darker gill margins or gills that stain on handling or from latex.

Tubes

The angular or rounded tube openings are called pores. Check if they are small (in which case you will need a lens to see them) or large. As with gills, pore colour may vary with age or on handling.

Flesh

Check the texture, colour and smell of the flesh above the gills/pores and in the cut stem.

Spore print

Spore colour is not readily ascertained in the field but it is relatively easy to determine from collected specimens, although mushrooms that are too young, too old or too dry will not produce a spore print.
A spore print is best set up as soon as you get home. Remove the stem and place the cap gills or pores on a sheet of glass or clear plastic or make prints on clear sticky-back plastic. Cover the cap to prevent it from drying out and leave it for three to four hours. If there is only a slight deposit, hold it up to the light to check its colour. Fix with hair spray or charcoal fixative.

must know

Like people, mushrooms can change their size, shape, colour, texture and smell as they mature, and spots and spines may wash off. It therefore pays to collect a range of developmental stages for identification purposes. Spore colour does not change, which is one reason why it is such a useful feature.

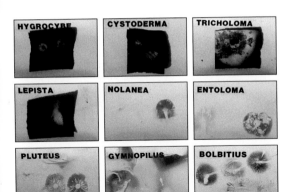

A range of spore prints, including white and various shades of brown.

Stem

Size
▶ What is the stem length and average width in centimetres?

Shape
▶ Is the stem hollow or solid, and is it cylindrical or flattened?
▶ Is the stem parallel-sided or tapering to and/or from the base?
▶ Is the stem base swollen?

Volva
▶ Is there a 'sac' or 'eggcup' around stem base?

Ring
▶ Is there the collar-like remains of the partial veil (absent in many species)?

Colour
▶ Is the stem the same colour as the cap or different?
▶ Is the stem colour different above/below the ring (if present)?
▶ Is the stem darker or lighter towards the base?
▶ Is the stem covered with darker/lighter fibres, scales or a raised network or zones?

Volva around stem base.

Ring high up stem.

Where do fungi grow?

Unlike green plants, fungi cannot make their own food. Instead, they are reliant on external food sources, and are often restricted to a particular type (*see* page 28).

must know

At its simplest, the place where an individual species lives is its habitat. The characteristics of a habitat include features such as its climate, soil type, topography and the living organisms present.

Experienced botanists or birdwatchers can make reliable predictions as to which species they will see based on knowledge of the habitat they are visiting. Most fungi, along with many plant and bird species, live only in certain habitats. For example, some fungi are restricted to pine woods on acid soils in the Scottish Highlands, while others are found solely on grassland in the south. So just as a birdwatcher wishing to see Waxwings may visit a habitat containing fruiting Rowan trees, on which the birds feed, an organised mushroom hunter searches for a particular fungus in a habitat rich in that species' required foodstuff.

At a broad level, this means looking for Field Mushrooms in grassland habitats or visiting woodland in order to find Ceps. There is, however, a range of different grassland habitats, including lawns, unimproved grazed pasture and grass managed for making silage. The variety of fungi these habitats contain varies considerably. Most species of fungi are inhibited by long grass, ploughing and reseeding, or by the addition of lime and inorganic fertilisers.

Mushroom hunters in the Peak District.

Of habitats and microhabitats

Certain habitats are defined by the presence of a particular dominant plant species. This is especially true of woodlands. Some fungi can be found in both Beech and Birch woods, while others are restricted to either one or the other. Beech, Birch and other native British broad-leaved trees such as Oak and Small-leaved Lime support a large fungal flora, while introduced broad-leaved species such as Sycamore and Horse-chestnut are much poorer in associated fungal species. Equally, fungal diversity is much greater in native Scots Pine woods than it is in forestry plantations of introduced conifers.

Within a woodland habitat there are hundreds of microhabitats. Some fungi are saprophytes, obtaining their nourishment from dead material such as fallen leaves, while others live on dead wood, including tree stumps and fallen trunks. Parasitic fungi may attack living trees, and their fruit bodies frequently take the form of bracket-like outgrowths from the trunk. Most of this latter group is found on only one (or a group of closely related) tree species.

Porcelain Fungus (*Oudemansiella mucida*) is typically found only on Beech trees.

Mycorrhizal fungi

There is another important way in which fungi can obtain food in a woodland habitat: many species form symbiotic relationships with trees. The fungal hyphae become integrated with the tree roots (mycorrhiza means 'fungus root'), from which they withdraw carbohydrates. Minerals such as phosphorus and potassium pass from the fungus to the tree, so that the relationship is of benefit to both partners.

Many common fungi form mycorrhizal relationships with just one or a limited number of tree species, although their fruit bodies develop from the ground with no obvious tree connection. Edible examples include the Orange Birch Bolete (*see* page 121), which is found only close to Birch trees.

Trees and shrubs in parks, gardens and hedges can play host to mycorrhizal fungi, though Ash is an exception, which is one reason why Ash woods are not the best mushroom-hunting grounds. Other fungi are associated with the roots of woody shrubs that are more typical of moorland and heathland habitats, including heathers and Bilberry.

The beautiful mycorrhizal Earthstar (*Geastrum triplex*).

must know

The underground spread of roots from a tree can stretch at least twice as far as its above-ground canopy. Be aware that this can result in supposedly woodland fungi appearing in grassland habitats such as meadows or lawns that are within rooting distance of trees.

Coniferous woodland with Scots Pine and Larch.

Fungi of coniferous woods

Of our three native conifers, Juniper, Yew and Scots Pine, only the latter forms extensive woodlands and most of these are planted. Pine has a large number of associated fungus species, but plantations of Spruce, Larch and other imported conifers are less fruitful hunting grounds for the mushroom hunter. Exceptions include slimy-capped species of bolete such as Slippery Jack (*see* page 124), which in addition to growing with our native Scots Pine is also found with some imported conifers. Larch Bolete (*see* page 124), also slimy-capped, is mycorrhizal with both European and Japanese Larch.

Many species of *Cortinarius* grow in coniferous woodland. These have a cobweb-like veil covering the young gills (*see* page 37) and a rusty-brown spore print. Some are poisonous, a few fatally so. Of the bracket fungi, Chicken of the Woods (*see* page 170) occasionally grows on Yew trunks. Wood Cauliflower (*see* page 174) grows near the base of pine trunks, while brightly coloured russulas, several orange-coloured milk caps (*see* page 140) and Brown Wood Mushroom (*see* page 90) all frequent the ground beneath coniferous trees.

Conifer stumps are home to Plums and Custard (*Tricholompsis rutilans*), named after its red-purple cap and orange-yellow gills; sadly, it is not edible.

Birch woodland.

Fungi of Birch woods

Birch woodland occurs on a wide range of acid soils, from dry heathland to wet, boggy sites. Birch is a good invader of disturbed ground, and as it is a fast-growing species it is frequently planted in gardens and around new buildings. As a result, some Birch-associated fungi are also common in urban situations. Birch trees rarely live longer than about 150 years as many are killed by the parasitic Birch Polypore (*Piptoporus betulinus*). The leathery fruit bodies of this species grow like thickened half-plates from Birch trunks, often many metres above the ground. The fungus was formerly used as a blade sharpener, hence its alternative common name of Razor-strop Fungus. Less common is the Hoof Fungus (*Fomes fomentarius*), which produces a much harder, thick, many-layered bracket.

A large number of fungi are mycorrhizal with the roots of Birch. The most spectacular of these is the red and white-spotted Fly Agaric (*see* page 73), which is also found under pine.

Woolly Milk Cap (*Lactarius torminosus*), with a fleece-like inrolled cap margin. The cut gills exude a milky juice. It causes gastric discomfort and diarrhoea if eaten.

Milk caps growing in Birch woods include the Coconut-scented, Ugly and Woolly species (*see* picture), the latter common in urban situations. Other Birch associates are the poisonous Brown Roll-rim (*Paxillus involutus*) and the edible Brown Birch Bolete and Orange Birch Bolete (*see* pages 121–122).

Fungi of Oak and Sweet Chestnut woods

While woodlands of our native oaks have many more species than are associated with Sweet Chestnut (which was introduced by the Romans), the trees are closely related and several bracket species occur on the living trunks and on stumps of both hosts. These include Maze-gill (*Daedalea quercina*), as well as the edible Chicken of the Woods, with a sulphur-yellow, cheesy-textured bracket (*see* page 170), and the aptly named Beefsteak Fungus (*see* page 168). Another edible is Hen of the Woods (*see* page 172), which grows at the base of Oak trees.

Oak stumps are the favoured habitat of Tufted Bell Cap (*Mycena inclinata*), while Oak Milk Cap (*Lactarius quietus*) is among the many mycorrhizal species to be found on the ground beneath the trees. The delicate, thin-fleshed Russet Tough Shank (*Collybia dryophila*) is common among Oak leaf litter, as are the Amethyst Deceiver (*see* page 149) and Lilac Bell Cap (*Mycena pura*), both of which are also found in Beech litter. Though Cep (*see* page 116) is not specific to Oak woodland, it is worth looking for the species in such habitats.

Oak Milk Cap (*Lactarius quietus*), a species found exclusively under Oak.

Mature Beech wood casting a dense shade.

Fungi of Beech woods

Although the dense shade cast by Beech trees makes an inhospitable environment for green plants, Beech woods contain a very diverse fungal flora. The beautiful Porcelain Fungus (*see* page 41) grows from the branches of older trees, while the related Rooting Shank (*Oudemansiella radicata*) emerges through the dead leaves from buried wood. Huge overlapping fawn brackets of Giant Polypore (*see* page 173) spread from Beech trunk bases and from the stumps of trees it has killed, while dead or dying Beech trunks are also favoured habitats of the Oyster Mushroom (*see* page 164). Search old stumps for the black, bogeyman-like Dead Man's Fingers (*Xylaria polymorpha*).

Edible species include Wood Hedgehog (*see* page 132) and the well-camouflaged Horn of Plenty (*see* page 134). Beech Milk Cap (*Lactarius blennius*) and Beechwood Sickener (*Russula mairei*) are common mycorrhizal species, as is Death Cap (*see* page 181), our most poisonous British fungus. Two other poisonous species include Lurid and Devil's boletes (*see* page 185), both with orange-red pores. For those prepared to dig for victory, the subterranean fruit bodies of Summer Truffle (*see* page 177) frequent Beech roots on well-drained soils.

Dead Man's Fingers (*Xylaria polymorpha*) on a Beech stump.

must know

Many of the best finds in Beech woods are not present in young plantations. Try to find a wood containing older trees, and with a good supply of stumps and fallen dead wood.

Fungi of mixed woodland

Many woods (apart from forestry plantations) contain a range of tree species, including conifers such as pines and larches, and native trees like Birch, Oak and Beech, together with Hawthorn, Rowan, Elder and Hazel. These woods will contain some of the specialist fungi described on the previous pages, along with a wide range of woodland fungi that are not restricted to any one of the tree species already listed.

On trunks and branches, look for Dryad's Saddle (*Polyporus squamosus*), King Alfred's Cakes (*Daldinia concentrica*; mostly found on Ash) and the edible Jew's Ear (usually on Elder; *see* page 162). Stumps and fallen wood are host to Honey Fungus (*see* page 156), the bitter-tasting Sulphur Tuft (*Hypholoma fasciculare*), edible Stump Puffballs (*see* page 114), the delicate Bonnet Bell Cap (*Mycena galericulata*) and the pink-spored Fawn Pluteus (*see* page 154). Terrestrial species include the Common Yellow and Blackening russulas and the related Charcoal Burner (*see* page 137), plus the larger Clouded Agaric (*see* page 150). Among the leaf litter, look for troops of Greasy Tough Shank (*Collybia butyracea*) and Wood Woolly Foot (*Collybia peronata*), and smell out Stinkhorn (*Phallus impudicus*). Mixed woods are also home to Wood Blewit (*see* page 97), boletes (*see* pages 116–125) and ink caps (*see* page 94), making them wonderful places for the mushroom hunter to visit.

King Alfred's Cakes (*Daldinia concentrica*) growing on Ash.

Upland sheep-grazed pasture.

Grassland fungi

In woodland habitats the species of tree is the main influence on the fungal flora, but for grassland, management is the key. British grassland habitats result from man's activities, including the original forest clearance and subsequent maintenance of a grass sward by grazing or cutting. Until the 19th century, most meadows, lawns, parks, graveyards and areas of downland were relatively long-term habitats receiving only organic fertiliser application, if any. The subsequent introduction of sown grasslands, maintained by heavy applications of inorganic fertiliser and lime, has resulted in some very boring habitats in the eyes of the mushroom hunter.

Some of the best grassland, in terms of the number of different fungal species present, is unimproved sheep-grazed pasture, much of which is found in hill-farming districts of Wales, northern England and Scotland. Most of this has never been ploughed, and the sheep (or cattle) dung also provides a home for dung-loving (coprophilous) fungi.

Among the more colourful grassland fungi are the small to medium-sized wax

must know

Some old graveyards are particularly rich in grassland fungi. Old lawns are also worth investigating – those surrounding Roecliffe Manor in Leicestershire have been designated an SSSI because of their fungi.

caps (*Hygrocybe* spp.). In addition to the edible Meadow Wax Cap (*see* page 106), the genus includes a range of white, yellow, orange and red species, along with the aptly named Parrot Wax Cap (*H. psittacina*) and less common Pink Wax Cap (*H. calyptriformis*). Grasslands also support a large number of small brown-capped fungi, including the black-spored mottle gills (*Panaeolus* spp.), a number of pink-spored species and the infamous Magic Mushroom (*see* page 70). Grassland fungi with a penchant for droppings include the Dung Round Head (*Stropharia semiglobata*) and Egg Shell Toadstool (*Panaeolus semiovatus*). The Fairy Ring Champignon (*see* page 104) also makes its characteristic mark on lawns and grazed grassland.

The larger edible grassland species include St George's Mushroom (*see* page 102), most frequent on chalk downland, the Field and Horse mushrooms (*see* page 85), Field Blewit (*see* page 96) and Lawyer's Wig (*see* page 94). Not all grassland fungi are mushroom-shaped. The tiny earth tongues (*Geoglossum* spp.) and matchstick-sized White Spindles (*Clavaria vermicularis*) are almost hidden in the grass, although the spherical (and edible) puffballs (*see* page 110) are more obvious.

Scarlet Hood (*Hygrocybe coccinea*) is a beautiful red wax cap.

good to know

Egg Yolk Fungus (*Bolbitius vitellinus*) grows on dead grass, so it turns up on hay, straw and compost heaps. A brown, cup-shaped *Peziza* also grows on old straw bales, while Split Gill (*Schizophyllum commune*), a formerly rare fungus of fallen wood, is now quite frequently observed where it has burst out through plastic-wrapped bales of hay.

Fungi of heathland and moorland

Lowland heathlands and the typically wetter (and more upland) moorlands are acidic habitats dominated by Heather. A group of fungi form root relationships with Heather and Bracken similar to those found associated with tree roots. Most of the fungi in these areas are small and are not on the menu for the edible-mushroom hunter. An exception is *Laccaria proxima*, which grows on damp acid soil among Heather and is a relative of The Deceiver (*see* page 148). A good place to look for it is by the ditches that line forest tracks in upland moorland. Its pinkish-brown cap expands to a diameter of 7cm (larger than that of The Deceiver), and it has flesh-coloured, widely spaced gills and a stem up to 10cm long. Though small, *L. proxima* grows in troops and so a handful can be collected very quickly.

Birch trees often become established on acid heaths and moors, where they attract species of associated edible fungi. Birch growing on wet *Sphagnum* (Bog Moss) is the specialised habitat for the Yellow Swamp Russula (*see* page 139), a good midsummer edible if you can get to it before the maggots.

Heather moorland in the Peak District.

Fungi of sand-dune grassland and slacks

The sand-dune systems found along our coasts are inhospitable for all but a limited number of plant and fungal species. The latter are mostly rare puffball relatives such as Winter Stalkball (*Tulostoma brumale*) and Sand Stinkhorn (*Phallus hadrianii*).

The often wet depressions situated between dunes are known as slacks. These are frequently colonised by low-growing willows, which support a range of mycorrhizal fungi, including species of russula and milk cap. These habitats are an Alice in Wonderland world, where the fungi are often taller than the trees.

The dry grassland on the landward side of a dune system is often rich in fungi, especially when it is grazed by Rabbits or farm stock. This is a habitat that often supports a number of edible species, including both Field and Horse mushrooms (*see* pages 85 and 87), St George's Mushroom (*see* page 102), Parasol Mushroom (*see* page 98) and several puffballs, such as the Meadow Puffball and the larger Mosaic Puffball (*see* page 110).

Brown Roll-rim (*Paxillus involutus*) is a poisonous woodland species, but is seen here growing with Dwarf Willow in a dune slack.

Leucocoprinus birnbaumii associated with exotic plants in greenhouses.

Fungi of urban habitats

One of the great delights of being a mushroom hunter is that long excursions into the countryside are not necessary. There is a remarkable diversity of fungi, including edible species, to be found in our towns and cities. Keep your eyes open while walking the dog, watching an amateur football match, strolling in a park, visiting a cemetery or even tidying the garden.

Gardens provide a range of specialised habitats for mushrooms. Lawns are home to the Brown Hay Cap (*Panaeolina foenisecii*), which appears as early as April; the Magic Mushroom (*see* page 70), fruiting from midsummer onwards; and the Fairy Ring Champignon (*see* page 104), the most common lawn edible. Garden trees (especially natives such as Birch, Beech and Oak) bring woodland fungi to your door, including Red-Cracked Bolete (*see* page 120), which is edible but has rather soggy flesh. Stacked logs are a habitat for Velvet Shank, a winter-fruiting edible (*see* page 160), while old compost heaps make a good home for Wood Blewit (*see* page 96) and even Giant Puffball (*see* page 108).

Pavements, car parks and school grounds are not as sterile as they look. Common Ink Cap (*see* page 95) is a frequent

In the last 60 years, gardens in southern England have played host to the Octopus Stinkhorn (*Clathrus archeri*), a native of Australia and New Zealand. How it came to Britain no one knows, but it is an attractive addition to any garden.

Redlead Roundhead on wood chip.

pavement-dweller, and Lawyer's Wig (*see* page 94) can be found beside car parks and on school playing fields. The aptly named Pavement Mushroom (*see* page 91) even grows through tarmac.

Old bonfire sites produce their own specialists, including the tiny orange discs of *Anthracobia macrocystis* and the Charcoal Pholiota (*Pholiota highlandensis*). Wasteland beside railway lines or canals is often invaded by Birch trees, and here, in addition to the famous Fly Agaric (*see* page 73), it is possible to find edible species. Make sure, however, that you avoid collecting any fungi from contaminated ground.

Cemeteries often harbour grassland species, including wax caps (*see* page 106), St George's Mushroom (*see* page 102) and, ironically, the Weeping Widow (*see* page 93). Other finds from wooded areas in cemeteries include Jew's Ear (*see* page 162).

The fashion for spreading wood chip as a mulch on gardens, parkland flower beds and children's play areas has resulted in a rise in the numbers of several previously infrequent species, including the inedible Redlead Roundhead (*Stropharia aurantiaca*). More usefully to those interested in edible species, the highly rated Black Morel (*see* page 128) is increasingly turning up among urban wood chip.

Black Morels on wood chip.

Edible or poisonous?

In 1891, Mordecai Cooke, the author of *British Edible Fungi: How to Distinguish and How to Cook Them*, commented in his preface that, 'Fungus eating is on the increase', later on in the book adding, 'The question is often propounded, is there no general rule by which good or harmless fungi can be distinguished from those that are deleterious?'

watch out!

Many edible fungi can be easily confused with poisonous ones. Do not rely on out-dated sources of information or old wives' tales.

Cooke's question was answered by the Director of Kew Gardens in his foreword to the 1945 edition of the Ministry of Agriculture and Fisheries' booklet *Edible and Poisonous Fungi*: '"rule of thumb" methods of distinction [between edible and poisonous fungi] are merely popular errors, some of which have persisted from the pre-Christian era'. The booklet described just 20 edible species, but included The Blusher (*see* page 183) without a warning that it can produce serious symptoms unless it is very well cooked. So beware older books about edible fungi!

Denis Benjamin, writing in 1995, commented rather more bluntly on relying on so-called common knowledge to identify fungi: 'The history of mushroom eating is littered with the corpses of those who followed the folklore of the day.' Interestingly, many similar myths relating to fungi are found all over the world, wherever fungi are collected from the wild.

Mushroom myths

Below are listed some old wives' tales concerning ways of distinguishing edible from poisonous fungi:

▶ The cap of a poisonous mushroom cannot be peeled. Not true – the red cap of the poisonous Sickener (*see* page 180) can be peeled.

▶ Cooking a poisonous species with a silver spoon blackens the spoon. Not true – silver is tarnished by hydrogen sulphide; there is no link between sulphur content and toxic chemicals.

▶ Fungi with a mild taste and smell are edible. Not true – the mild-tasting False Morel (*see* page 129) can be fatal.

▶ Fungi collected from grassland are safe. This myth first appears in the writings of the Roman poet Horace (65–8BC): 'Fungi which grow in meadows are the best, it is not well to trust the rest.' Not true – the very poisonous Sweating Mushroom (*see* page 186) grows in grassland.

▶ Poisonous fungi are brightly coloured, while white ones are edible. Not true on both counts – the edible Chanterelle (*see* page 130) is bright orange, while the fatal Destroying Angel (*see* page 182) is white.

▶ All mushrooms growing on wood are safe. Not true – some wood-rotting *Galerina* species (*see* page 183) are highly poisonous.

▶ Poisonous mushrooms can be made safe by parboiling. Not always true – the toxins in Death Cap (*see* page 181) are not destroyed by heat.

▶ Drying a fungus destroys its toxic contents. Not true – dried Magic Mushrooms (*see* page 71) and Fly Agarics (*see* page 74) remain hallucinogenic.

▶ All fungi that exude a milky fluid from the damaged gills are poisonous. Not always true – the Saffron Milk Cap (*see* page 140) is edible.

Cep with tooth marks.

▶ Fungi that change colour on handling are poisonous. True for the Yellow-staining Mushroom (*see* page 86), but false for Bay Bolete (*see* page 118).
▶ A mushroom eaten by an animal must be safe. Not true – Rabbits and Grey Squirrels both eat Death Cap (*see* page 181) without apparent ill effect.

Rules for mushroom hunters

▶ Never eat a mushroom unless it has been carefully identified as an edible species. Check each fruit body; don't assume that a collection of similar-looking specimens are all the same species.
▶ Be aware of the poisonous lookalikes that can be confused with edible species.
▶ Be careful if collecting edible species in other countries where there may be similar-looking poisonous species that are not found in Britain.
▶ Do not eat specimens that are old, infested with insect larvae or going mouldy. Keep fungi in the fridge and consume them within 48 hours of collection.
▶ Do not collect mushrooms from contaminated land such as the sides of main roads, old factory sites or landfill areas. Fungi accumulate heavy metals, other toxins and radioactive materials, especially caesium-137 (although contrary to alarmist reports, levels of the latter in British fungi as a result of the 1986 Chernobyl accident are well within safe limits).
▶ Do not eat wild collected species raw – some fungi contain poisons that are destroyed by heat and so can only be safely eaten when cooked.

Cep with a mould covering the pores.

- ▶ If you are trying a species for the first time, eat only a small portion and don't mix it with other species.
- ▶ Inform guests if you are serving wild fungi. Some people are allergic to species of mushroom that most people find edible and safe.

Rules to ensure the safe collection of fungi

- ▶ Make a note of the habitat (grassland, under trees, on dead wood and so on – *see* pages 40–53).
- ▶ Collect the whole fruit body, especially the stem base (and surrounding volva, if present).
- ▶ Note any unusual smell, surface texture or colour that may fade before examination at home.
- ▶ Note any colour change/fluid discharge after handling the cap/stem or cutting the gills/flesh.
- ▶ Do not collect underdeveloped ('button stage') fruit bodies as these are difficult to identify accurately.
- ▶ Once you are home, take a spore print (*see* page 39) and confirm identification with a reliable book.

Shaggy Ink Caps growing beside a road – not a good place to collect fungi.

Preserving edible fungi

Faced with both feast and famine, our ancestors developed ways of preserving food. Along with more modern methods, these traditional techniques allow mushroom hunters to avoid waste and enjoy the fruits of their labours throughout the year.

> **watch out!**
>
> Accurate identification of species that are to be preserved is very important. Remember that some species can cause adverse symptoms in a minority of the population (for details, see under each edible species listing), and so these should not be included in the preparation of extracts, ketchups and so on where these may be served to guests whose susceptibility to such species is not known.

As with sun-dried tomatoes, preserved mushrooms exhibit different flavours, aromas and textures to those of fresh ones. Prior to preserving, always discard mouldy or maggoty specimens and brush or wipe clean the others.

Drying mushrooms

A kilogram of fresh mushrooms has a shelf life of only a few days; in the dried state, however, the same quantity will weigh about 100g and will keep for years. Choose whole, small mushrooms, or thinly slice larger ones. Using wire or string, thread the fungi like a pearl necklace, with a gap between each one, and hang above a radiator or in an airing cupboard for several weeks. Alternatively, put them on a baking tray in a fan-assisted oven at 80°C or in a cool range, with the door ajar. For stockists of mushroom driers, *see* page 23, or you can make one yourself with wire racks and a light-bulb heat source.

Dried St George's Mushrooms.

The best species for drying are Cep and other boletes, Morels, Horn of Plenty, Fairy Ring Champignon, Jew's Ear, St George's Mushroom, Wood Cauliflower and Chanterelle.

A tin of powdered
Cep and a plate
of home-made
mushroom powder.

Keep dried mushrooms in airtight glass or plastic containers.
They can be reconstituted by soaking in lukewarm water (or
wine if the recipe calls for it) for 20 minutes. Strain the liquid
and keep it for stock. Milling dried mushrooms in a coffee
grinder provides a seasoning that can be added to many meals.
This is the best way of using Curry-scented Milk Cap (*see* page
145) and Aniseed Toadstool (*see* page 151).

Mushroom extract

▶ To 500g of chopped ink caps, wax caps,
  older boletes or *Agaricus* mushrooms
  (don't waste Chanterelles or morels), add
  300ml of water, 300ml of red wine, 60ml
  of soy sauce and a teaspoon of salt.
▶ Simmer for 50 minutes, then strain
  through a nylon sieve.
▶ Return the liquid to the heat and boil
  until reduced by half.
▶ Pour into sterilised, screw-top glass jars.
  The extract keeps in the fridge for up to
  eight weeks, or longer if frozen into ice
  cubes.

Mushroom ketchup

▶ Sprinkle 100g of salt on at least 1kg
  of chopped and mashed mushrooms.
▶ Cover and leave to stand for two to
  three days.
▶ Add 300ml wine vinegar, half a
  finely chopped onion, and a teaspoon
  each of ground cloves, allspice and
  peppercorns.
▶ Boil briefly, then simmer for two
  hours until most of the liquid has
  evaporated.
▶ Strain through a nylon sieve and bottle in
  sterilised jars.

Freezing mushrooms

Young specimens of Cep and other edible boletes, along with *Agaricus* mushrooms, blewits, St George's Mushroom and Wood Hedgehog, can be frozen raw. Saffron Milk Cap needs blanching (put into boiling water for two minutes, then place immediately into ice-cold water) and drying first. Label and date all bags and consume within a year. Unless you are using the frozen fungi in soups, do not thaw them before cooking. Instead, immerse them in boiling, salted water until just soft, then dry them and use as if fresh. Try deep-frying frozen fungi without thawing them.

Pickling mushrooms

Preserving mushrooms in a strong salt or acid medium prevents them from spoiling in storage. For salting, use fresh, sliced mushrooms, immersing them in a brine solution (20g of salt to

Buttered mushrooms

Most fungi keep better if cooked before being frozen. Simply slice and fry species such as Cep, Chanterelle and Chicken of the Woods in plenty of butter for ten minutes (150g butter to 500g of mushrooms). Pack in containers, cool, then freeze.

Duxelles

This mixture is an ideal starting point for many soups, stuffings and fillings:
► Sauté a couple of finely chopped shallots and garlic cloves in 50g of unsalted butter.
► Add 500g of finely chopped mushrooms (any edible species or a mixture) and 50ml of vegetable stock or wine.
► Cook until the liquid has reduced well, then add chopped herbs to taste.
► Either store in a fridge for up to five days or freeze as ice cubes.

100g of mushroom) in glass jars. Store in a cool place. Even after careful washing, however, many find the end product too salty.

In Britain, most people prefer to pickle mushrooms in vinegar (the acetic acid acts as a disinfectant) and store them in olive oil. Although this masks the original flavour, it maintains the colour and texture:

▶ Ensure that only firm, clean mushrooms are used, and slice larger ones.
▶ Place 500g of fungi in a mixture of 250ml of wine vinegar (this imparts a better flavour than malt vinegar), 100ml water, a tablespoon of salt, four black peppercorns, two cloves, half a cinnamon stick and a clove of garlic.
▶ Boil for eight minutes, drain, cool and ladle into clean, sterilised screw-top jars. Cover with olive oil.

Pickled mushrooms are a wonderful accompaniment to pasta dishes, but remember that once opened the jar must be stored in a fridge and the contents consumed within a few days.

Small, highly coloured mushrooms such as Chanterelles and Amethyst Deceivers can be blanched, dried and then bottled whole in vodka. Jars of these make wonderful Christmas presents.

The cultivation of edible fungi

Although wild-mushroom collectors still employ hunter-gatherer techniques, to ensure a continuous supply of fresh food certain species of mushroom are cultivated. Today, the annual worldwide production of edible fungi exceeds 4 million tonnes.

Wood-ear (*Auricularia cornea*), a close relative of Jew's Ear (*see* page 162), grows on decaying wood and its cultivation in China goes back more than 1,300 years. Despite being cultivated, demand outstripped supply, and a century ago huge quantities of wild-collected Wood-ears were exported to China from New Zealand. Today, Wood-ear is a staple ingredient of oriental cooking and is cultivated on a large scale in China, Japan and Taiwan. Traditionally, the species is grown on cut logs, but these are now being replaced by plastic tubes containing sawdust and other vegetable waste. Dried Wood-ears can be purchased from oriental food shops.

Fresh cultivated fungi.

The more mushroom-like Shiitake (*Lentinula edodes*) grows wild in the Far East on dead wood of oaks, chestnuts and hornbeams. It, too, has been cultivated in China and Japan for more than a thousand years.

Traditional methods of cultivating Shiitake mirror those used for producing Wood-ear. Living trees are felled, left for two months and then sawn into logs, into which the fungus mycelium is

introduced in a series of drilled holes. Fruiting does not start for 18 months, but it continues after this for up to six years. Cultivation of Shiitake in China is close to 100,000 tonnes a year and results in the annual felling of 100,000 trees. Modern methods include growing the fungus on enriched sawdust, a technique that involves a wait of only seven weeks prior to cropping and now used by a number of British growers supplying fresh Shiitake for the home market. Sliced Shiitake makes a great addition to a stir-fry along with garlic, ginger and soy sauce, also a fungal product.

Another edible fungus with an equally long history of cultivation in the Far East is *Flammulina velutipes*. This is often called by its Japanese name of Enokitake, but we know it wild in Britain as Velvet Shank (*see* page 160). Cultivated under low light conditions, it produces a tiny convex cap on the end of a very long thin stem. It can now be bought fresh in Britain.

Paddy Straw Mushroom (*Volvariella volvacea*) has been grown for centuries on bundles of damp rice straw. It has a cup-shaped sheath (volva) at the stem base and is available dried or canned. However, its rather glutinous texture is not to everyone's taste.

British mushroom hunters have long enjoyed the fruits of the native wood-rotting Oyster Mushroom (*Pleurotus*

Close-up of fresh Enokitake.

**Cultivated Pink
Oyster Mushroom
(*Pleurotus djamor*).**

ostreatus), but in the last 30 years this (and a range of related species) has become available as commercially grown 'wild mushrooms'. Our native species (*see* page 164) is typically a grey-blue colour (hence its name), but among those being cultivated is the yellow-coloured *Pleurotus citrinopileatus*, originating in the Far East, and a pink variety of the tropical species *Pleurotus djamor*. They are easily cultivated on sawdust, straw and even cotton waste.

The cultivation of mushrooms in Europe dates back only as recently as the 17th century, although the ancient Greeks did grow a wood-rotting species in a manner similar to the methods used in the Far East for Shiitake. In 1699, English diarist John Evelyn commented that mushrooms were being raised artificially 'in France, by making an hot bed of Asses-dung, and when the heat is in Temper, watering it well impregnated with the Parings and Offals of refuse Fungus's'. The techniques used in France were originally developed there for growing melons outside.

Only later were mushrooms grown indoors, and Joseph Banks (1743–1820), founder of the Royal Horticultural Society, was one of the first people in Britain to own a mushroom house. At about the same time, production of mushrooms in disused stone quarries beneath Paris heralded the start of large-scale production of *champignons de Paris* – the Cultivated Mushroom (*Agaricus bisporus*).

By the end of the 19th century, the Americans had initiated a system of cultivating *Agaricus* mushrooms in sheds. This modern system, brought up to date in the 1970s, now produces more than 70,000 tonnes of mushrooms in Britain. Most of these are strains of the Cultivated Mushroom, originally collected for cultivation from horse dung and manured fields but now an uncommon species in the wild. Contrary to popular opinion, it is not the same species as the Field Mushroom (*see* page 92).

In the wild, the cap of *Agaricus bisporus* is covered with small brown scales, as were all cultivated mushrooms before a mutant, non-scaly white strain arose in 1927. This has since become the most commonly grown form of the species. One place still growing the brown form, now sold as Chestnut Mushrooms, is Bradford-on-Avon, where the mushrooms are produced in caves originally created by the extraction of limestone.

In recent years, a whole range of locally cultivated fresh edible species have been made available to the British public from specialist 'farms'. These include blewits, sold under the French name *Pieds Bleus* (*see* page 96), and Lion's Mane (*Hericium erinaceus*). Even Black Truffles (*Tuber melanosporum*; *see* page 177) can now be cultivated on trees inoculated with mycelium. So although the white mushroom is still king, it no longer rules on its own.

Button mushrooms ready to be harvested.

want to know more?

The largest mushroom museum in Europe is at Saumur in the Loire Valley, southwest of Paris. Situated in old limestone caves, the museum includes plenty of information in English and provides the chance to see mushrooms being cultivated.

Growing your own

For mushroom hunters frustrated by a dearth of finds during a long, dry summer or in the cold winter months, and for those who feel buying so-called exotic mushrooms goes against the grain, there is a middle path – home cultivation.

The first mushroom-growing kits that became available were largely restricted to the production of white strains of *Agaricus bisporus*, the mushroom most widely sold in shops. In the past these have not been very effective, but today both the technology and the range of species that can be grown has expanded, in many cases mirroring the increased range of species on sale in shops.

Details of suppliers of spawn and mushroom kits can be found on page 23. Those still wedded to *Agaricus bisporus* can purchase wooden trays filled with wheat straw compost that has been inoculated with the mushroom spawn (mycelial threads). With the simple addition of water, such kits will start supplying fruit bodies after about three weeks and can continue for up to three months.

Kits that have been inoculated with Oyster Mushroom are also available, but a cheaper method involves purchasing the spawn and a bag of straw separately. Oyster Mushroom is one of several species that can be grown on mushroom logs into which spawn has been introduced. These can be placed indoors or in a garden, but they must be kept moist.

For those who are happy to collect their own logs and drill them with holes, small dowel plugs inoculated with spawn can be purchased to push into the holes. The optimistic gardener can even purchase wheat grain inoculated with the spawn of fungi such as Wood Blewit and Shaggy Ink Cap to enhance their list of garden produce.

want to know more?

If you are seriously interested in growing your own mushrooms, the excellent book *Mushrooms in the Garden* by Hellmut Steineck is highly recommended. Despite the title, it gives clear advice on growing a range of edible fungi both in the garden and indoors. (Publication details can be found on page 189.)

Growing Oyster Mushrooms

▶ Purchase Oyster Mushroom spawn plugs (*see* page 23).
▶ Sterilise glass jars by microwaving them for 5 minutes.
▶ Add three parts of powdered wheat grains, twelve parts of vermiculite (available from garden centres) and four parts of water to the jars.
▶ Cover the jars and leave them at room temperature for 10–20 days.
▶ Transfer the contents to clear plastic mugs with holes cut in the side.
▶ Place in a well-lit, high-humidity chamber such as old aquarium, and spray the walls with water twice a day.
▶ Just over a week later, the fungi should start to appear.

You can experiment with other spawn plugs using this method.

Shiitake growing on a cut log.

What's in a mushroom?

As recently as the 1990s, a book on edible wild mushrooms stated that in terms of nutritional value, fungi had little to commend them, containing few nutrients and even fewer vitamins. This merely served to bolster popular belief that mushrooms were good only for those on a diet.

must know

Fungi appear on our plates in forms other than the fruit body. Marmite is a yeast (fungus) extract particularly rich in B vitamins. Quorn, meanwhile, is a protein food made from the mycelium of a fungus. It is being used increasingly in the production of meat-free foods.

As with many vegetables, fresh mushrooms contain about 90 per cent water and only 4-5 per cent carbohydrates, including a little glucose but mostly chitin, a substance that adds fibre to the diet. A 300g portion of mushrooms (before the addition of butter or oil) contains just over 100 calories; an average portion is more like 40 calories. Less than 1 per cent of mushrooms is fat, and most of this is the essential, unsaturated linoleic acid.

More importantly, mushrooms contain protein levels similar to those of peas and beans. There are also vitamins in fungi, though the quantities of these vary with the species. They are a good source of the B group, especially B2, niacin, folic acid and B12, the latter often missing from vegetarian diets. In addition, Chanterelles contain carotene, a precursor of vitamin A, and a little vitamin D. Fungi also contain minerals such as potassium and phosphorus, plus significant amounts of zinc and selenium.

Mushrooms and medicine

Historically, herbal medicine has included the use of fungi in addition to plants. For example, the mature stage of puffballs, with their mass of spores, was used to help stop bleeding, while Jew's Ear infusions were utilised to help alleviate sore throats.

The former use of mouldy fruit or bread to treat wounds (in some areas using a special bun baked on Good Friday) has been given a scientific explanation since the discovery that a chemical produced by such moulds has mild antibiotic properties. The development of the commercial production of penicillin from species of the mould *Penicillium* during the 1940s heralded the introduction of other fungus-based antibiotics.

For hundreds of years, midwives used small amounts of the Ergot fungus (*see* page 75) to stimulate childbirth and to ensure complete expulsion of the afterbirth. Now obtained from laboratory-grown culture, ergometrine is still used during childbirth. Ergotamine, another ergot-derived chemical, helps to alleviate migraine headaches. Other important drugs of fungal origin include cholesterol-lowering acids and the cyclosporins; the latter suppress the immune system and lower the chance of rejection after organ transplant.

Smouldering amadou, made from thin strips of Hoof Fungus (*Fomes fomentarius*) seen here growing on Birch, impregnated with saltpetre, was used to cauterise wounds.

> **did you know?**
>
> A mushroom originating from Brazil (*Agaricus blazei*) and cultivated in Japan under the name Royal Agaricus is said to stimulate the body's manufacture of interferons, thereby helping to increase resistance to viral infections. It is also being used as an alternative treatment by some cancer patients.

Hallucinogenic fungi

Mushroom hunting used to be considered a harmless if rather eccentric pastime, but now a new band of mushroom hunters is being viewed with more suspicion.

watch out!

Some of the Magic Mushroom lookalikes contain other toxins and their ingestion can result in hospitalisation.

The change was initiated in 1957 by Gordon Wasson, a retired American banker. After an examination of the religious and recreational use of hallucinogenic mushrooms in Mexico and other parts of central America, he wrote an article in *Life* magazine entitled 'Seeking the Magic Mushroom'. Unintentionally, this helped to fuel the 1960s counterculture in the USA, famously recalled by Timothy Leary's plea to 'turn on, tune in and drop out'. The mushrooms concerned are *Psilocybe mexicana* (the 'p' is silent) and other species of the genus, which all contain the hallucinogenic alkaloids psilocybin and psilocin. The structures of these chemicals are similar to lysergic acid,

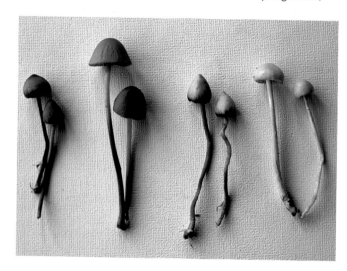

A collection of similar-looking little brown mushrooms; the Magic Mushrooms are the third pair from the left.

produced by the Ergot fungus (*see* page 75) and the basis for LSD, another powerful hallucinogen that was also embraced by the hippie generation.

It was not until the 1970s that the British discovered the hallucinogenic effects of their own *Psilocybe semilanceata*. This little brown fungus has a narrow cone-shaped cap (hence its traditional name of Liberty Cap), purple-black spores and a wavy stalk that turns blue at the base after picking.

A common fungus, especially in unimproved sheep-grazed pasture, *Psilocybe semilanceata* also occurs on playing fields and lawns (my own included). As the British discovered that the fungus induced auditory and visual hallucinations while also enhancing the senses of touch and smell, so its common name changed from Liberty Cap to Magic Mushroom.

The chemicals found in Magic Mushroom were deemed to be class A drugs under the Misuse of Drugs Act 1971, but possession of the mushrooms was not considered an offence unless they were made into a preparation. This became a grey area, as argument raged over whether dried mushrooms represented a preparation. In 2002, the Home Office indicated that it was not an offence to possess, sell or consume a freshly picked *Psilocybe*, and this paved the way for the opening of Amsterdam-style 'shroom' shops in Britain. These began selling fresh, cultivated Magic Mushrooms and kits for growing a range of non-native species of *Psilocybe*. By early 2005, the Home Office countered by claiming that cultivating, packaging, weighing and labelling created a preparation, and the Drugs Act 2005 made the mushrooms a controlled drug, a potential concern for landowners.

Plate of dried Magic Mushrooms.

Of toads, witches and religion

For hundreds of years mushrooms have suffered from a bad press in Britain. Authors have either ignored them or linked them with themes of death and decay. D.H. Lawrence, in comparing the bourgeois to a mushroom, wrote, 'what a pity they can't all be kicked over like sickening toadstools'.

The Common Toad.

The English word toadstool, used to describe any inedible (and by inference, poisonous) mushroom, first appeared as 'tad stole' more than 600 years ago. The link with toads is widespread: one Welsh name for a poisonous fungus translates as 'toad's cheese', while there is a Danish name meaning 'toad's hat' and a French one meaning 'toad's bread'. Our Common Toad (*Bufo bufo*) also has a link with poison, in this case its venom-containing skin glands. The venom causes irritation of the mucous membranes in the mouth and nose, besides having local anaesthetic and hallucinogenic properties. The latter is caused by the alkaloid bufotenine, a chemical also detected in some of the poisonous *Amanita* toadstools. Toads figure in many ancient folk remedies, and together with toadstools they were represented in medieval artistic interpretations of hell.

One of the witches in Shakespeare's *Macbeth* refers to 'paddock', the Scottish name for a toad, and Propertius, a Roman poet, mentions toads as part of the witch's brew used to ensnare men for sexual pleasure. Witches were even believed to be capable of transforming themselves into toads. Common names for some toadstools remind us of their association with witches and also with fairies – Witches' Butter (black rather than yellow) and Fairies' Bonnets are two common examples. The young stage of

the impudent Stinkhorn (*Phallus impudicus*) is known as a witch's egg. Virtuous middle-class Victorian ladies destroyed any Stinkhorns they found, so that maidservants wouldn't be corrupted by the sight of the mature 'member'.

There is no direct evidence that British witches used toadstools as part of their flying potion, but shamans (and others) from parts of Siberia and Lapland do consume the red and white-spotted Fly Agaric (*Amanita muscaria*). This distinctive fungus contains the toxins muscimol and ibotenic acid, which cause the senses to become heightened and lead to feelings of drunkenness. Mordecai Cooke's 1862 publication *Plain and Easy Account of the British Fungi* described the inebriated state that follows ingestion of the carefully prepared toadstool, listing symptoms such as erroneous impressions of size and distance. This book is the likely source for the fictional mushroom that produces the same effects when eaten by Alice in Lewis Carroll's 1865 classic.

Cooke's account of Fly Agaric consumption says, 'The property is imparted to the fluid excretion of rendering it intoxicating, which property it retains for a considerable time.' Fluid excretion is a polite

The mature Stinkhorn's 'member'.

Fly Agarics.

phrase for urine, meaning that inebriation also results if you drink the urine of someone who has eaten a Fly Agaric. This has since given rise to the term 'getting pissed', now linked with the effects of alcohol.

Knowledge of the antics of the Fly Agaric-fuelled shamans from the reindeer-herding Saami tribes of Lapland is thought to have inspired another author, Clement Clarke Moore. His poem, first published in 1823, begins 'Twas the night before Christmas'. It transforms the saintly, sober, horse-riding St Nicholas into an inebriated, fur-clad figure flying high on a sleigh pulled by reindeer. The origin of the red and white colour of the modern-day Santa's coat may owe more to the red and white mushroom than to the advertising campaign of a well-known fizzy drink. For a more detailed account of this, see my book *The Magic of Christmas* (2004).

The image of the Fly Agaric has also infiltrated children's literature, including the form of Noddy's house in Enid Blyton's classic stories.

watch out!

Although it is rarely fatal, Fly Agaric contains chemicals that can cause nausea and diarrhoea (*see* page 182). It is not recommended as a casual inebrient, especially if you do not know how to prepare the fungus before ingestion.

Some authors have promoted Fly Agaric as soma, worshipped by the Aryans people and central to their scriptures, the Rig-Veda, more than 3,000 years before the birth of Christ. Settling in the Indus Valley in about 1500BC, the Aryans held beliefs that are thought to be among the roots of Hinduism. On the other side of the world, in Central America, stone statues of fungi dating from as early as 500BC indicate the importance of the early ritual use of mushrooms in the New World.

In parts of Europe, the effects of mind-altering fungal chemicals were not limited to the deliberate ingestion of fungi as part of religious or social rituals. A German document dating from AD857 records that 'a great plague of swollen blisters consumed the people with a loathsome rot, so that their limbs were loosened and fell off before death'. During the Middle Ages, incidents of St Anthony's fire (whose symptoms include a burning sensation in the limbs) were commonplace throughout Europe. Seeking an explanation to the cause of their problems, people turned to blaming witches.

Ergot growing on a grass flowerhead.

Modern research indicates that most witchcraft trials from the 16th to the 18th centuries took place in regions that grew Rye as the staple food, and that poor summer weather (indicated by narrow widths in dated sequences of tree rings) preceded the majority of the trials. We now know that the symptoms of St Anthony's fire are caused by a tiny fungus called Ergot. This infects cereal grains (especially Rye in wet weather), and its poisons are spread when it is ground, along with the grain, into flour. Today, ergotism in cereals is contained by using varieties that are partially resistant to the fungus and by screening the grain samples.

did you know?

Ergotism was not restricted to Europe. The early colonists who settled in the Salem region of Massachusetts took Rye seeds with them to grow as their cereal crop. Diary records from the early 1690s indicate unusually cold, wet spring weather. Ergot (as with most fungi) is more prevalent in moist conditions, and it now seems likely that the 1692 witch trials were the direct result of Ergot poisoning.

Where have all the mushrooms gone?

Senior citizens frequently inform me that there were more mushrooms in the 'old days'. Although this is hard to verify (unlike birds and plants, we don't have enough accurate records), some species of fungi do appear to have declined over the last 50 years.

Where this decline involves edible species, there has been the inevitable charge that their increased collection from the wild has resulted in a demise in their numbers. A similar decline has been noticed in many of Britain's butterfly species, but these are not collected for food. A range of experiments conducted in Europe and America involving edible fungi have shown no decline in the total weight of fruit bodies produced as a result of regular picking. Instead, the decline in fungal numbers can be traced to loss of habitat, increased pollution from acid rain, and the use of nitrogen fertilisers and chemical weedkillers. Habitat loss has been most serious in relation to ancient woodland and unimproved grassland.

While there is no evidence that picking mushrooms causes them to become less common, there is concern that selfish and commercial collectors may trample rare plants and remove potential food sources for insects and mammals. One result of this concern has been the passing of by-laws (most famously in the New Forest) banning commercial collecting.

People collecting only a limited number of edible species are unlikely to collect any rare fungi. Some 'rare' species may actually be more

Pink Wax Cap.

Hericium coralloides, a close relative of *Hericium erinaceus*, which is now cultivated under the name Lion's Mane.

common than we think – when Plantlife asked its members to send in records of the easily identifiable Pink Wax Cap (*Hygrocybe calyptriformis*), previously recorded from fewer than 50 sites in Britain and on a list of endangered species, 200 new sites were recorded! The endangered species list also includes Devil's Bolete (*see* page 185), which has recently been found to be locally common in many southern counties of England. The beautiful, edible and very rare *Hericium erinaceus* is also on the list, although the species is now being cultivated (*see* page 65).

Code of conduct

For the mushroom hunter collecting for personal use, several organisations have produced a code of conduct for responsible collecting. Among the more important points of these are:

► Follow the Country Code.
► Minimise damage to plants, leaf litter and soil.
► Remove dead wood only if this is needed to identify a particular fungus.
► Take a good field guide with you and try to identify at least some species (e.g. inedible or poisonous species) without collecting them.
► Do not collect fungi you do not intend to eat.
► Pick no more than 1.5kg per visit and no more than half of the fruit bodies of any single species.
► Do not collect unexpanded mushrooms as they will not have discharged any spores.

3 Edibles found in open habitats

This chapter portrays those edible British species that are found in open habitats such as grazed pasture, meadows, playing fields, lawns and churchyards together with species of roadsides, pavements and disturbed ground. Some species of mushroom (*see* page 89), blewit (*see* page 96) and parasol (*see* page 98) are more frequent in woodland habitats but are included in this section along side their field-based relatives.

Which mushroom is it?

For those who have restricted their collecting to the Field Mushroom (*Agaricus campestris*) and its larger relative the Horse Mushroom (*Agaricus arvensis*), it may come as a shock to learn that there are similar but poisonous species of mushroom.

Many older collectors remember finding more mushrooms in their youth. As outlined on page 76, anecdotal stories of the decline in wild mushrooms over the last 50 years are difficult to prove, but there is plenty of evidence pointing to the destruction of the habitats favoured by Field and Horse mushrooms. Both species grow in grassland, and as saprophytes (*see* page 28) they require nutrient-rich soil, usually in the form of animal dung or silt from flooded rivers. This not only provides the necessary nutrients, but it also helps to keep the soil moist, which is needed for the production of their fruit bodies. Since World War II, many suitable sites have been built on or have been ploughed up and used for growing arable crops.

Additionally, relatively few fields now receive their fertiliser solely in the form of horse dung, which is preferable, if not essential, for the Horse Mushroom. Grassland where nitrogen

A ring of Horse Mushrooms in grazed pasture near Abbotsbury, Dorset.

and other nutrients are provided through the addition of
chemical fertilisers, and where weedkillers are applied, is
typically devoid of mushrooms. Changes in agricultural practice,
including the installation of more efficient land drains, have not
favoured the growth of wild mushrooms either. Furthermore,
mushrooms fruit through the summer and early autumn, so
Britain's increasingly dry summers may also be affecting the
number of fruit bodies produced.

Many people gather only Field Mushrooms or Horse
Mushrooms in the belief that by avoiding other fungi they are
safe from being poisoned. Both of these species belong to the
same genus, *Agaricus*. Members of this genus have easily
recognised features, including free gills (*see* page 37) that start
off pink, changing to brown and finally black as they mature and
disperse their chocolate-brown spores. All have a ring on the
stem and most have fleshy caps. What is less certain is just how
many different species of *Agaricus* mushrooms there are in
Britain, although current research indicates at least 40 and
there may be many more. Not all species of *Agaricus* inhabit
grassland – some edible species grow in woodland, and others
are urban-dwellers, occurring in parks, gardens or even on

A mushroom showing
the main features of
Agaricus: free gills
(pink when young
then brown), ring and
a button stage, where
a veil covers the
immature gills.

pavements. More importantly, however, not all *Agaricus* species are edible.

While the identification of the Field Mushroom (*see* page 85) and Horse Mushroom (*see* page 87) is relatively easy, this is not the case for all members of the genus. In particular, mushroom hunters need to be aware of the poisonous *Agaricus* species, especially Yellow-staining Mushroom (*see* page 86). Be warned – characters such as size, cap colour, the presence or absence of cap scales, and ring shape vary between individuals of the same species and even in the same individual as it ages. These are problems with all fungi but are particularly pronounced when dealing with *Agaricus* species.

In fact, many species of *Agaricus* are relatively uncommon (though some are under-recorded because of difficulties with identification). Based on records held by the British Mycological Society, the most frequently recorded *Agaricus*, starting with the most common, are: Field Mushroom; Horse Mushroom; Wood Mushroom (edible); Red-staining Mushroom (edible); Yellow-staining Mushroom (poisonous to some); The Prince (edible); and Pavement Mushroom (edible). Among the less common species in the wild is the Cultivated Mushroom (*Agaricus bisporus*), which occasionally turns up on rich, disturbed soil.

Beware of imposters. *Leucoagaricus leucothites* can be distinguished from the *Agaricus* mushrooms by the fact that it has white gills and spores.

Unlike all other *Agaricus* mushrooms, this species bears its spores in twos, not fours, although this can be ascertained only with the help of a high-power microscope.

Several edible *Agaricus* species grow on dune grassland, while Bernard's Mushroom (*Agaricus bernardii*) was formerly restricted entirely to seaside pastures with a high salt concentration from sea spray (it even has a fishy smell). Increasingly, it is being found on road verges contaminated with the salt spread on roads during icy weather.

Unfortunately, the most common poisonous member of the genus, Yellow-staining Mushroom, can occur in a variety of habitats, wherever there is rich soil. It grows in grassland, open woods, gardens, parks and even cemeteries, but is not deadly poisonous. Assuming you have found an *Agaricus* species with pink free gills, chocolate-brown spores and a ring on the stem, check out the following characters to help you decide if you have one of the common edible species.

Bernard's Mushroom, with its characteristic cracked cap and cut flesh that stains purplish pink on exposure to air.

Smell of the gills

▶ Field Mushroom – smells like a shop-bought mushroom.
▶ Horse Mushroom, Wood Mushroom and The Prince – all smell more like bitter almonds, marzipan or aniseed.
▶ Pavement Mushroom – has a slightly sour smell.
▶ Yellow-staining Mushroom – smells of ink. It is the ink-smelling phenol in the mushroom that makes it poisonous (the same is true for other species with a similar smell), a problem made worse by cooking.
▶ Red-staining Mushroom – has very little aroma.

Colour of cut flesh above the gills and in the stem

▶ Pavement Mushroom – shows little change.
▶ Field Mushroom – slowly flushes pale pink.
▶ Red-staining Mushroom – turns reddish brown.
▶ Horse Mushroom, Wood Mushroom and the Prince – turn slightly yellow (pink appears in the Prince stem base).
▶ Yellow-staining Mushroom – cut flesh in *stem base* turns bright (chrome) yellow.

Chrome-yellow cut stem base in Yellow-staining Mushroom.

Colour of the cap surface after handling

▶ Field Mushroom and Pavement Mushroom – show little change.

▶ Horse Mushroom – bruises ochre-yellow.

▶ Wood Mushroom – bruises pale yellow.

▶ Yellow-staining Mushroom – bruises bright yellow.

▶ The Prince and Red-staining Mushroom – the caps of both are covered with brown fibrous scales.

The cogwheel pattern on the underside of the ring in a Horse Mushroom.

Size and shape of the ring

▶ Field Mushroom – the ring is simple, thin, white and transient.

▶ Horse Mushroom – the ring is thick (double layered), with a cogwheel pattern on the underside.

▶ Wood Mushroom – the ring is simple, often torn and grey-brown beneath.

▶ Yellow-staining Mushroom – the ring is large and downturned, with cottony patches beneath.

▶ Red-staining Mushroom – the ring is large, simple and grey-brown.

▶ The Prince – the ring is large and floppy (stem woolly below).

▶ Pavement Mushroom – the ring is double, with the lower part often upturned (erect).

Field Mushroom

Field Mushroom (*Agaricus campestris*) is the most well known of our wild edible fungi, but it is not always correctly identified. Many other edible fungi described in this book, which some people would call toadstools, are much easier to recognise.

Field Mushrooms occur in short grassland on rich soil, especially on grazed pastureland but also in parks, on lawns, on playing fields and on golf courses where the grass is kept short by mowing. They fruit at any time from late May through to November, especially after wet weather, and usually occur in small clusters, sometimes as fairy rings.

Young specimens (the button stage) are nearly spherical, with a smooth white cap and bright pink gills covered with a white veil. As the fleshy cap expands, its margin remains inrolled until maturity, when the flat cap may exhibit concentric rings of pale brown scales. The cap rarely exceeds 10cm in diameter.

The closely spaced gills are free (they don't reach the stem) and change from deep pink through

Field Mushroom, button stage.

How to cook Field Mushrooms

Field Mushrooms, especially when mature, are stronger in flavour than cultivated mushrooms and can be used in all recipes that call for the latter. Young ones have a firmer texture but less flavour. Old specimens need to be checked for maggots, and very old specimens have black, rather watery gills, although this is not a problem if they are made into soup.

Young Field Mushrooms can be sliced and eaten raw in salads; there is no need to peel them and you can use the stems as well as the caps. If you want to cook Field Mushrooms, they are best fried for just a few minutes at a high temperature with a minimum amount of oil or butter.

Older specimens are especially good for making mushroom ketchup (*see* page 59).

If you are collecting Field Mushrooms, make sure that your specimens have pink (or brown in the case of older mushrooms) free gills and a chocolate-brown spore print. If you are near trees, check out the dangerous lookalikes described in the 'must know' box on page 89.

brown to black with age. The gills have a pleasant 'mushroomy' smell. The short, chunky, white stem bruises faintly brown with handling and bears a small, simple, white, transient ring. The white flesh in the stem and above the gills in the cap may stain faintly pinkish red on cutting.

Apart from the other edible *Agaricus* species, the Field Mushroom is most easily confused with Yellow-staining Mushroom (*Agaricus xanthodermus*). In contrast with the Field Mushroom, the centre of the

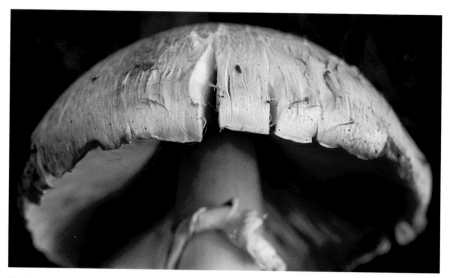

Distinctive yellow bruising (resulting from handling) on the cap of a Yellow-staining Mushroom.

During April and May, grassland habitats are also home to the white-capped St George's Mushroom. This good edible fungus is described on page 102, and has white gills and spores, no ring and a mealy smell.

immature cap of *A. xanthodermus* is flat-topped and the young gills are greyish white. Older specimens smell unpleasant, and the white cap and stem easily bruise bright yellow, as does the cut stem base. About 20 per cent of people who eat Yellow-staining Mushroom suffer diarrhoea and sickness for up to 48 hours, which, while not life-threatening, is avoidable.

Horse Mushroom

Horse Mushroom (*Agaricus arvensis*) has a long history of cultivation and is still sold in some food shops, although nothing beats the thrill of finding this large fungus in the wild.

Surprisingly, some people still treat it with suspicion, probably because it does not smell like a Field Mushroom and the cap bruises yellowish brown on handling.

Rarer in the west and north of Britain, this summer to early autumn species is usually associated with grassland that is grazed by horses or cattle, although it also grows on disturbed ground. The creamy-white, hemispherical button stage is typically nearly as large as an expanded Field Mushroom. The white veil covering the immature gills cracks into a cogwheel pattern surrounding the stem and is left as remnants at the cap margin. The smooth, or finely scaly, convex cap has an inrolled edge until maturity, when it can attain a diameter of up to 20cm. Older caps have a faint yellow tinge and slowly bruise yellowish brown with handling.

The young, thick, free gills are greyish white, but later turn pink and finally very dark brown from the spore colour.

Horse Mushrooms, the young hemispherical caps showing faint yellow patches.

How to cook Horse Mushrooms

This is a very large, thick-fleshed mushroom. William Withering, the 18th-century physician who investigated the medicinal properties of Foxglove, recorded a Horse Mushroom weighing 14lb (6.4kg). As with many species, older specimens are more likely to be maggot-ridden, so check before carrying them home.

The thick, firm flesh of the Horse Mushroom, which discolours yellow on cutting, has a nutty taste that many prefer to that of the Field Mushroom. Open caps are excellent when brushed with oil and grilled (or baked), gill side up. Cover the partially cooked caps with a diced mix of the mushroom stems, together with onion, tomato, pepper, pine nuts and seasoning.

watch out!

Horse Mushroom, like Wood Mushroom and The Prince, is an accumulator of heavy metals, including cadmium. It is thus important to avoid collecting Horse Mushrooms from busy road verges or industrial areas where the land may be contaminated.

must know

The similar *Agaricus urinascens*, also known as *Agaricus macrosporus* is another very large, domed, edible mushroom with a faint aniseed smell. It is more common in northern hill pastures and open woodland as well as on coastal grassland in Scotland.

They smell strongly of aniseed or bitter almonds. The long, white stalk bruises yellow and bears a large, persistent double ring. The flesh at the base of the stem does *not* yellow when cut.

From a distance, Horse Mushrooms can be mistaken for Giant Puffballs (*see* page 108), but the only potentially serious lookalike, as with the Field Mushroom, is the Yellow-staining Mushroom (*see* page 86). Unlike the Horse Mushroom, however, the Yellow-staining Mushroom has a very different (inky) smell, is less chunky, and both the bruised cap and the cut flesh in the stem base quickly turn *bright* yellow.

Mature specimen of Horse Mushroom, with yellowish-brown bruising on the cap. Note the veil remnants at the margin.

Woodland mushrooms

There are several quite common edible *Agaricus* species that grow in woods. Of these, Wood Mushroom is white-capped and similar to the grassland species, while others, including Red-staining Mushroom, have caps covered with brown scales and look less like a typical mushroom.

Wood Mushroom (*Agaricus silvicola*) is comparable to a slimmer version of the Horse Mushroom (*see* page 87). Unlike its relative, however, Wood Mushroom grows from rich soil under either broad-leaved or coniferous trees. It is relatively common in the East Midlands and southern England, but rarer in the north and west of Britain.

Unlike other *Agaricus* mushrooms, the Wood Mushroom has a rather thin-fleshed cap that soon flattens as it expands to a diameter of 5–10cm. The smooth cap is creamy white with pale yellow overtones and it darkens with age. White areas of the cap bruise yellow on handling. The tall, smooth, slender, white, hollow stem bruises yellow like the cap and is rarely more than 2cm in diameter, except at its bulbous base. The simple pendulous ring has a ragged appearance and a grey-brown underside.

Wood Mushroom growing in a Birch wood.

must know

The similar yet poisonous Yellow-staining Mushroom (*see* page 86) can also occur in woods, but it does not smell of aniseed, instead having an unpleasant inky aroma. Like the Wood Mushroom it stains yellow on bruising, but additionally the cut flesh at the stem base turns chrome yellow.

When collecting woodland mushrooms you must also make sure that their fruit bodies do not have white gills or a white spore print, and that the stem does not emerge from a bag-like volva. Both the highly poisonous Death Cap and Destroying Angel (*see* page 181) are similar in appearance to Wood Mushroom, but they have white gills and emerge from a volva.

Red-staining Mushroom showing brown cap scales and reddening flesh on its damaged stem.

The young pinkish-grey gills of the Wood Mushroom mature to a greyish brown and smell strongly of aniseed. The cut white cap flesh slowly yellows, while that in the stem base turns brown. Wood Mushroom can be substituted in recipes for Cultivated Mushrooms but has a much richer flavour.

Red-staining Mushroom (*Agaricus silvaticus*), also known as Brown Wood Mushroom, is one of Britain's most common *Agaricus* mushrooms and usually grows in coniferous woods. The very similar Bleeding Brown Mushroom (*Agaricus haemorrhoidarius*), typically found under broad-leaved trees, is now considered by some authorities to be the same species. Both are edible, so I will consider them together here as Red-staining Mushroom.

Unlike the Field Mushroom, Red-staining Mushroom has a brown cap covered with darker scales or fibres and often merges with its leaf-litter background. The pale stem has a bulbous base and a thin floppy ring that is brown on the underside. The odourless pink gills have a reddish tinge and mature dark brown. The most distinctive (and to some people offputting) feature of the Red-staining Mushroom is that the white flesh in both the cap and stem quickly turns red on exposure to air. Despite this, it is edible, although of only mediocre flavour.

Urban mushrooms

While both Field Mushrooms and Horse Mushrooms are occasionally found in town parks and even on garden lawns, for three other species of *Agaricus* the majority of records are from urban rather than rural habitats.

Pavement Mushroom (*Agaricus bitorquis*) is a species of compacted ground, often fruiting beside paths, roads and on pavements, squeezing between paving stones or even pushing up through tarmac. In this respect, it is like the Common Ink Cap (*see* page 95), with which it also shares a long fruiting season – from spring through to autumn.

Pavement Mushroom, showing the double ring on the stem.

The smooth, dirty-white to pale ochre-coloured cap is about the size of that of a Field Mushroom, and is usually flattened at the centre but convex near its inrolled margin. The rather sour-smelling, crowded gills are initially a pale pink, before maturing dark brown. The white stem has an unusually thick double ring, the upper part spreading out while the lower one remains more erect and sheath-like. The firm white flesh does not discolour when cut. Pavement Mushroom is a good edible species, although it is prone to suffering from traffic pollution and dog urine!

A young specimen of The Prince, showing the white woolly scales at the stem base.

The Prince (*Agaricus augustus*) is most likely to turn up in ones and twos in parks and gardens, although it also grows in woods. It occurs in grass alongside coniferous hedges and especially under the shade of Yew trees. This beautiful mushroom has a large (up to 20cm in diameter) white cap speckled with concentric rings of russet-brown scales. The white veil remnants are often left hanging from the cap margin.

The stem, which extends well into the ground, is covered with white woolly scales below a large floppy ring. The gills have a pleasant almond smell and the cut flesh stains faintly yellow. This is a meaty mushroom with a strong almond flavour – it was a favourite of a particular Roman emperor, hence its scientific name. Sadly, The Prince is not common, but don't overlook it if it does turn up in your garden.

Cultivated Mushroom (*Agaricus bisporus*), besides being common in greengroceries and supermarkets, can occasionally be found on roadside verges, compost heaps and other sites where rich soil has been disturbed. The wild form usually has a cap covered in small brown scales, more like the Chestnut variety available in shops. Flower beds enriched with spent mushroom compost are also likely to produce a short-term display of Cultivated Mushrooms.

Cultivated Mushroom – Chestnut variety.

Weeping Widow

Ignored by many books on edible mushrooms, the Weeping Widow (*Lacrymaria velutina*) is worth looking out for after wet weather any time from May to November.

It is one of the few edible species with a black spore print (apart from the Shaggy Ink Cap), and grows among grass in a variety of habitats, including pastures, playing fields, parks, woodland rides and road verges. Like the ink cap, with which it often grows, it is also common in urban situations. It usually grows in small groups.

The fleshy, dull brown cap is deeply convex when young, retaining a central hump as the fungus ages, and is streaked with darker, radiating fibres. Initially, the gills are protected by a white, cobweb-like veil. As the cap expands, however, the veil disintegrates, leaving a ring zone on the stem and fragments at the cap margin. In moist weather the crowded, adnate, brown gills exude a few tear-like droplets that darken with the black spores. Mature gills are mottled black and brown but retain a white edge.

watch out!

Don't confuse Weeping Widow with species of *Psathyrella*, which can be differentiated from the former by their smooth caps, slender, brittle stems and lack of cobweb or mottling on the gills.

In this picture you can see water droplets exuded from the gills and the remains of a veil.

How to cook Weeping Widows

As with ink caps, only young Weeping Widows are worth collecting. Discard the hollow fibrous stem and cook the caps on a high heat. Be prepared for lots of black juice, which will make a strange-coloured sauce. The slightly bitter flavour is loved by some and hated by others.

The ink caps

Ink caps can easily be separated from all other fungi by their black spores and deliquescent caps, in which the gill tissue autodigests (dissolves) into an inky-black fluid after the spores have been released.

must know

Search for Shaggy Ink Caps on playing fields, grass verges, lawns, arable field margins, by woodland paths and in urban situations. They may even be found pushing up through pavements and car-park boundaries.

There are over 100 species of ink cap in Britain. Some species are less than 2cm across and grow in large troops on tree stumps, while others develop in small numbers from horse dung. However, one of the largest is the Shaggy Ink Cap (*Coprinus comatus*), also known as Lawyer's Wig. It is usually found growing in groups on grassland from buried organic material.

Shaggy Ink Cap – note that the cap base is dissolving into an inky-black fluid.

How to cook Shaggy Ink Caps

The delicate texture and salty flavour of the Lawyer's Wig make it an excellent edible mushroom. The main problem is that the process of deliquescence, which usually takes several days, accelerates to just a few hours after picking. Prevent this by picking young ones (before the stem is visible) and cook them as soon as possible.

Slice each fruit body in half vertically through the cap and stalk. Preheat a pan with a tiny quantity of oil or butter, and add the cut halves, gill surface down. Cook for less than a minute before turning to brown the other side for 20 seconds.

Ink caps are wonderful on bread or as a pizza topping, or you can try coating portions with batter and deep-frying them. Slow-cooked older specimens are less appetising, resembling hot slugs. These can, however, be put in a blender and added to stock to make an excellent, if rather odd-coloured, soup.

watch out!

Do not eat Common Ink Cap unless you are teetotal. The unpleasant symptoms, which may result in hospitalisation, can occur even if alcohol is consumed several days before or after the fungus meal. The American name for the species is Tippler's Bane, which serves as a good warning.

Common Ink Cap.

The beautiful, uncommon Magpie Ink Cap (*Coprinus picaceus*) among Beech leaf litter.

Torpedo-shaped and apparently stalkless when young, the predominantly white cap of the Shaggy Ink Cap breaks up into tiers of scales so that it resembles a lawyer's wig – hence its other common name. Mature specimens can reach a height of 30cm, and as the gills turn from white, through pink to black, the base of the cap dissolves into black droplets, revealing the slender, tapering, hollow stalk. Look for them as early as April, and all through the year to December, after any warm, wet spell of weather.

Common Ink Cap (*Coprinus atramentarius*) frequents similar habitats to its shaggy relative. It is shorter and broader, its bell-shaped, fawn-grey cap lacks large scales, and it is slow to reach the inky stage. This species is edible, but it contains a chemical that prevents the breakdown of acetaldehyde in the body, which itself is produced when alcohol is drunk. The resulting symptoms include diarrhoea, an increased heart rate and a metallic taste in the mouth.

The blewits

Apart from Field and Horse mushrooms, hardly any other wild fungi have regularly been sold in Britain until recently. Blewits are an exception to this, and have long been available from market stalls, especially in the Midlands.

Blue they are not, but the colour purple is a feature of the two common species. Unlike the *Agaricus* mushrooms, blewits lack a ring. Field Blewit (*Lepista saeva*) is a medium-sized (cap to 12cm across), occasional, autumn-fruiting fungus of pastures, parkland and woodland edges, where the undulating grey-brown, smooth caps are often hidden among the surrounding vegetation. The sinuate (with a nick close to the stem) pale, flesh-coloured gills produce spores of a similar colour. The firm flesh has a mealy odour and a pleasant taste. The short, thick stem is often swollen at its base, where it is suffused with lilac-purple streaks, giving rise to local names such as Blue Stalk or Blue Leg.

Field Blewit is now cultivated and is one of an increasing number of edible species grown for the restaurant trade. Its firm flesh and strong flavour make it a particularly good addition to casseroles.

must know

Look for Field Blewit from September to November. Observe the coloured stem base to confirm its correct identification. St George's Mushroom (*see* page 102) also smells of meal and has a fleshy, if paler, wavy-edged cap, but it lacks the coloured stem base and fruits three to four months earlier.

Field Blewit – note the inrolled cap margin and purple swollen stem base.

How to cook Wood Blewits

Wood Blewits often grow in rings and their thick flesh provides rich pickings for the mushroom hunter. Older specimens tend to be watery and full of maggots, so try to collect young ones during dry weather. On no account should Wood Blewit be eaten raw, as it contains chemicals (mostly destroyed by heat) that cause digestive upsets or rashes in susceptible people.

Finely slice the tough stems before adding them to the caps for frying or stewing. The rather slimy flesh, with its strange perfume-like taste, goes well with leeks and onions. Some people even liken it to eating tripe, a dish still served in the area where wild blewits are sold. Young specimens pickle well, and Wood Blewits can be frozen for later use, although you should cook them before freezing.

watch out!

The spore colour of Wood Blewit is a very pale pink in contrast to similar-looking poisonous fungi, including violet species of *Cortinarius*. The latter have rusty-brown spores and a cobweb veil protecting the young gills (*see* photograph, *bottom right*).

Wood Blewit with cylindrical stem, inrolled cap margin and violet, sinuate gills.

Wood Blewit (*Lepista nuda*) is more common than its field cousin. It grows among vegetation in broad-leaved and coniferous woods, as well as in parks and gardens, not always near trees. When young, the cap, stem and especially the gills show a lilac hue, but on ageing the cap turns to tan, the stem colour fades and the gills turn pinkish brown. Confusingly, it is this species that is often sold as Blue Legs or under its French name of *Pied Bleu* (meaning 'blue foot'). Rarely seen before mid-September, it continues up to Christmas and even during the early months of the new year.

Cortinarius sp., showing the cobweb-like veil covering the young gills.

Parasol mushrooms

The Parasol Mushroom (*Macrolepiota procera*) was formerly traded at Covent Garden and is my favourite edible fungus. It scores highly on both quantity and quality. The unusually dry-textured cap is rarely maggot-infested and it has a wonderful flavour.

must know

The edible Slender Parasol (*Macrolepiota gracilenta*) is slightly smaller than the Parasol Mushroom and has a less scaly cap (especially near the margins). It inhabits grassy places and is typically found in coastal regions.

Parasol Mushroom is an infrequent species of grassy pastures, roadside verges, orchards, parkland and open, broad-leaved woodland. Typically, five or six will occur quite close together and sometimes they produce large fairy rings. The only downside to this fungus is its rather short season – usually from midsummer to autumn.

A young specimen, before the cap expands, resembles a pale brown hen's egg on a short stalk. The stalk later elongates up to 30cm and, as the cap develops, it becomes more convex and later flat, save for a raised, brown, central region. Around this, the creamy-beige cap colour is patterned with bands of darker, cottony scales. Specimens with caps measuring up to 25cm across are not uncommon.

Parasol Mushrooms – the deeply convex young specimen shows the pattern of scales. Note the darker, raised central region on the mature specimens.

The thick, crowded, creamy-white gills of Parasol Mushrooms (the spore colour is also white) are free of the slim, hollow stem, which is largely cylindrical but noticeably wider at its bulbous base. Below the large, double ring (which can be eased up and down the stem without being broken), the beige-coloured stem is covered with brown, snake-like markings. The creamy-white flesh of the cap and stem does not discolour when cut.

Shaggy Parasol (*Macrolepiota rhacodes*) is a commoner species than the ordinary Parasol Mushroom and is more often associated with woods and shrubberies where there are conifers. It can even be found under coniferous hedges or individual conifers in parks or gardens, despite the dryness usually associated with such habitats. It also frequents compost heaps.

With a smaller but more chunky cap (usually up to 15cm across), the Shaggy Parasol bears larger, more fibrous cap scales that curve up at their edges. These vary in colour from grey to chestnut brown. The creamy-white free gills bruise reddish brown and slowly age a similar colour, although they produce white spores.

Parasol Mushroom showing cap scales, double ring and snake-like markings on the stem.

A fairy ring of Shaggy Parasols near a woodland edge.

3 Edibles found in open habitats

must know

From above, the scaly form of Yellow-staining Mushroom (*see* page 86) can be taken for a Parasol Mushroom, but it has pink gills.

Shaggy Parasol, which in comparison to Parasol Mushroom shows fewer, larger scales with upturned edges, and a stem without snake-like markings but reddening towards the asymmetrically swollen base. Note the orange-red tones in the cut flesh of both cap and stem.

Tufted fruit bodies of Shaggy Pholiota at the base of a Rowan tree.

The shorter, stockier, cream-coloured stem of the Shaggy Parasol is often asymmetrically swollen at its base. It lacks the snake-like markings of Parasol Mushroom but ages and bruises reddish brown, especially near its base. The white flesh in the cap and stem turns orangey red on cutting and has a strong, slightly sweet smell (in contrast, Parasol Mushroom has no distinctive odour).

The only other common large woodland fungus with brown scales on its cap is the Shaggy Pholiota (*Pholiota squarrosa*). Unlike the Shaggy Parasol, however, it grows in dense tufts attached to rotting wood at the base of broad-leaved trees. It also differs in having yellowish-brown gills, a brown spore print and shaggy scales on the basal part of the stem below the ring. Its bitter-tasting flesh is not edible.

How to cook parasols

Many older books on edible fungi give equal prominence to both the Parasol Mushroom and Shaggy Parasol, but more recent evidence shows that consumption of the latter does not agree with everyone. For a minority of the population, the after-effects of eating Shaggy Parasol include gastric upset, headache and skin rash. For this reason alone, it is important to be able to distinguish between the two species. Those foraging for themselves should also try just a small quantity of Shaggy Parasol at the first tasting. If, like me, you are free of any side effects, then you can continue to enjoy both of these parasol species, but remember not to serve Shaggy Parasol to those who have not previously eaten it without adding a health warning.

Parasol caps are edible nuggets but the stems are usually very tough and so should be discarded. When still immature and cup-shaped, the caps are best baked in the oven with a stuffing of leek, breadcrumbs and parsley, topped with a knob of butter.

Simply frying the flat caps is another wonderful way to enjoy their nutty flavour. However, remember that their prized dry texture can be ruined by the absorption of too much oil or butter. Dipping cap segments in milk or egg and coating them with oat flakes or oatmeal before frying ensures a crisp exterior and a flaky interior. For a more interesting approach, try battering small pieces and deep-frying them. If you take home more than you can eat within a day or two, slice the caps thinly and dry them for future use.

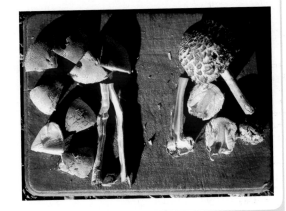

Parasols on the chopping board prior to cooking. On the left is Slender Parasol and on the right Shaggy Parasol.

must know

When collecting parasols near trees, be aware that deadly poisonous species of *Amanita*, including Panther Cap (*see page 182*), also have white free gills, a white spore print and a large ring on the stem. Some also have spots on the cap surface. *Amanita* species differ from parasols in the presence of a volva at their stem base and in their cap colour.

St George's Mushroom

Even the most dedicated mushroom hunter finds the first three months of the year largely lacking in edible finds. Morels (*see* page 126) are classic early season fungi but are seldom encountered by the novice collector, unlike that other herald of spring, the St George's Mushroom.

must know

Very few other large mushrooms fruit as early as the white-spored, white-gilled St George's. Early fruiting Field Mushrooms can be distinguished from St George's in that they have pink gills and dark brown spores. In May, beware early fruiting specimens of the poisonous Red-staining Inocybe (*see* page 184), which has yellow gills that, like the cap and cut flesh, bruise red and smell of rotting fruit.

Books written before the 1990s indicate that *Calocybe gambosa* typically put in an appearance on or shortly after St George's Day (23 April), hence its common name. By the start of the 21st century, however, sightings in March had become regular occurrences in southern counties of England, and as I write this on 13 April 2005 in Sheffield, I have a collection of fresh specimens on the table. St George's Mushroom is at its best in May, but is rarely found fresh after the end of June.

The species has a preference for soils over chalk or limestone but is catholic in the range of habitats it frequents. It is most common in grassland, especially on chalk downs or dune swards, but also grows on road verges (limestone chippings are often used in road building), graveyards (guess where the calcium comes from), lawns and playing fields. Additionally, it is a mushroom of shrubberies, hedgerows and woodland edges. Rarely solitary, it usually grows in fairy rings.

The domed, fleshy cap of St George's Mushroon has the feel of damp leather and grows to 12cm across, initially with inrolled edges. The cap, crowded sinuate gills and broad, solid stem are all creamy white but become tan brown and drier with age. Older caps are often misshapen, flatter and with wavy, split margins. *Calocybe* has the distinctive smell of freshly milled flour or dough.

How to cook St George's Mushrooms

Young fruit bodies are extremely heavy for their size. Slice their moist flesh (cap and stem) and put in a pan of browned, chopped onions to stew for five to ten minutes. Add stock, lemon juice or white wine, and finally yogurt or cream and a garnish of parsley. Don't be put off by the mealy smell, as this largely disappears on cooking.

Older specimens (often odourless) can be sliced and fried in butter, but don't overcook them or they will become tough. Young ones can be sliced thinly and eaten raw in salads. Some people find St George's Mushrooms difficult to digest, so try a small amount for your first tasting. The early fruiting season results in a mushroom that is rarely maggot-infested – another plus.

St George's Mushroom in short grassland – note the crowded, white gills.

Fairy Ring Champignon

Of all the grassland fungi that regularly produce their fruit bodies in rings, the most common is the Fairy Ring Champignon (*Marasmius oreades*). It borrows the French name for mushroom, although in the north of England 'champignon' has been corrupted to 'champion'.

did you know?

Fairy rings were once thought to be caused by the activities of Moles, Toads and lightning strikes. However, they are now known to represent the growing edge of the underground fungus mycelium, from which the fruit bodies are produced.

It is found on lawns, parks and among short-grazed grassland. An anonymous Victorian writer set the scene:

The nimble elves
That do by moonshine green sour ringlets make
Whereof the ewe bites not; whose pastime 'tis
To make these midnight mushrooms.

The 'green sour ringlets' of taller grass betray the presence of this mushroom even in the winter months when it is not fruiting, as does the adjacent circle of shorter (or even dead) grass, so hated by lawn fanatics. *Marasmius oreades* is a very small mushroom, but it has endeared itself to ardent mycophiles because hundreds

Fairy Ring Champignon living up to its name.

watch out!

The poisonous Sweating Mushroom or Fool's Funnel (*see* page 186) also grows in rings among short grass. It differs from Fairy Ring Champignon in that it has creamy-white, *crowded* gills that are fully attached (and even run down) to the non-pliable stem. Its caps are often depressed at the centre.

Close-up of *Marasmius oreades*, showing the pale tan, widely spaced, adnexed gills and short intermediate gills.

can be gathered from one circle, it is easily dried, it has a rich flavour and it has a very long fruiting season – from April through to the November frosts. The mushrooms can be found in the same locality each year after wet weather, although they may not appear during very dry summers.

The small (3–5cm) bell-shaped caps of Fairy Ring Champignons soon flatten, save for a darker, raised central area. Buff brown and smooth when moist, the cap dries paler to a creamy-tan and takes on a wrinkled, leathery appearance. The similar-coloured stem is only the thickness of a drinking straw but is pliable and not easily broken. The creamy-buff gills, which are barely attached to the stem, are well spaced and interspersed with short intermediate gills near the cap margin. They produce a white spore print. When fresh, the mushrooms smell of newly mown hay.

How to cook Fairy Ring Champignons

In France, these mushrooms are eaten raw, thus preserving their firm texture and nutty (almond) flavour. Lightly fried in olive oil, they make a fine hors d'oeuvre, but they are principally used to flavour soups and stews – the traditional English steak and kidney pie benefits from their addition.

The caps (discard the tough stems) are very easy to dry, by simply threading them on cotton and hanging them up in a warm place. They keep dried for a long time and quickly reconstitute in warm water, when they can be used to add a rich flavour to any dish. *Marasmius oreades* is also an excellent source for making dried mushroom powder (*see* page 58).

The wax caps

Britain's north–south split can even be detected in the writings of mycophiles. Richard Mabey, Peter Jordan and Antonio Carluccio, all based in southern England, have largely ignored the Meadow Wax Cap.

After 25 years spent foraging in the Peak District, Cumbria, Wales and Scotland, I feel it is time to redress the balance!

Meadow Wax Cap (*Hygrocybe pratensis*) is one of the commonest members of its genus, most of which are more frequent on lawns and unimproved short grazed grassland in areas of above-average rainfall in northern and western Britain. It is larger (up to 10cm across and 8cm high) and more robust than most of its relatives. Initially convex, the fleshy cap later flattens (save for a central hump) to the shape of a child's spinning top. It is then easy to see the thick, well-spaced waxy gills that run down

must know

Look for Meadow Wax Caps from August to November. They are often found growing in rings. False Chanterelle (*see* page 131) is a similar size, shape and colour, but has narrow, crowded gills and a slim stem. It typically grows on heathland or under conifers. It is not worth eating and may cause digestive upset.

Meadow Wax Cap, showing the thick orange decurrent gills and paler stem.

Snowy Wax Cap (*Hygrocybe nivea*).

onto the stout stem, which narrows at its base. Between the gills at the cap margin are shorter intermediate gills, while bridging them all on the cap undersurface is a network of horizontal veins. The apricot-tan colour of the cap and gills ages to pale buff, the colour of the stem.

Most of the other wax caps are too slimy or insubstantial to be worth eating. The Snowy Wax Cap (*Hygrocybe nivea*) is a white species that is typically smaller and more thin-fleshed than the Meadow Wax Cap, with which it often grows. This, too, is edible, but it is not recommended as beginners find it difficult to distinguish from a species of *Clitocybe* that contains muscarine, a dangerous poison (*see* page 186).

Giant Puffball

In 1877, the world's largest Giant Puffball (*Calvatia gigantea* or *Langermannia gigantea*) was recorded in New York state, USA. It had a diameter in excess of 1.6m, and from a distance was taken to be a sheep resting on the grass.

good to know

Look for Giant Puffballs in early summer – by late autumn most have gone brown and are past the stage when they are fit to eat.

There are many different species of puffball, most of which are spherical, lack a stem and have a thin skin surrounding the spore-bearing tissue. The skin ruptures at maturity, releasing clouds of brown spores. Our ancestors likened this process to farting – 'Fist Ball' and 'Fuss Ball' are two older names for puffballs that imply this link. The fart connection is even apparent in *Lycoperdon*, the scientific name for the genus containing the smaller puffballs, which comes from two Greek words meaning 'wolf fart'.

Typically the size and shape of a football, but with a diameter upwards of 20cm, Giant Puffballs grow in small groups or as fairy rings among grassland, at woodland edges, under hedges and in

Giant Puffballs.

gardens from early May to early autumn. The fungi reoccur for many years on the same site. Favouring rich soil such as old rubbish tips or among nettles, they can be confused with sheep, other puffballs or plastic footballs.

watch out!

Some people find puffballs difficult to digest, so don't eat large amounts on the first occasion. Beware of the spores from older, brown puffballs as they can cause breathing problems.

How to cook Giant Puffballs

As with other puffballs, *Calvatia gigantea* is edible only when young – it must be white, firm and heavy (a medium-size one will weigh about 5kg). Giant Puffballs don't keep well after being picked, so put them in the fridge when you get home and if possible consume within a few hours of collection. They are not easy to preserve either, but they are a good excuse for a party! Cut the ball in half using a carving knife. The fungus should have a thin skin and a firm, white, rubbery, marshmallow-like texture. If it is soft and showing tints of yellow or brown, it is too old. Maggots do not infest these fungi, but centipedes often make shallow burrows near the surface – shake them out prior to cooking.

I cut thin slices ('steaks'), which I fry in hot butter until crisp on each side. Puffballs absorb a lot of fat; this can be prevented by dipping the slices in egg or milk and then coating them with oatmeal prior to frying. Alternatively, dip pieces in batter and deep-fry them. The rather delicate taste (some liken it to sweetbreads) is much enhanced by lemon juice and garlic.

For those with a big oven, slice the top off the puffball and hollow out the remainder like a Hallowe'en pumpkin. Dice the flesh and fry it with chopped shallots, chestnuts, parsley and pre-soaked sun-dried tomatoes. Place this stuffing back in the shell and put the lid on. Cover with strips of bacon, wrap in foil and bake in a moderate oven for 50 minutes.

Half a young Giant Puffball, showing the thin skin and firm, white flesh.

The smaller grassland puffballs

Although they are less spectacular than the Giant Puffball, there are a number of smaller species of puffball, some of which frequent grassland habitats. As with all puffballs, these are edible at the young stage, when they are firm and white inside.

Martin holding two Mosaic Puffballs.

must know

To prepare and cook Mosaic Puffballs, follow the information given on page 109 for Giant Puffballs. However, you should discard the sterile base and the thick skin before cooking.

The largest of these species is the Mosaic Puffball (*Handkea utriformis* or *Calvatia utriformis*). It is most common on grazed grassland in more upland parts of Britain, but also occurs in coastal areas on sandy grassland. With a diameter of up to 15cm, it is often mistaken for a small specimen of Giant Puffball. It differs in that its shape is more flattened (it is always broader than it is tall) and it narrows slightly to a furrowed base.

The surface of very young Mosaic Puffballs is covered with an outer skin that cracks into a pattern of pyramid-shaped scales. Later, these fall off, leaving a mosaic pattern on the thicker, inner skin. The lower region (which does not form spores and so is called a sterile base) may persist for several years. Look for Mosaic Puffball in the autumn; it typically fruits later in the year than its relative the Giant Puffball.

Other grassland puffballs are more the size and shape of golf balls, but they are still worth collecting for the pot. They sometimes occur on golf courses but are more often found on short grazed grassland, heathland and even on lawns. Meadow

Puffball (*Vascellum pratense*) is like a small version of the Mosaic Puffball. Its flattened, creamy-white fruit body is initially covered with tiny scales, but these wash off to leave a smooth skin. A cross-section reveals that the stalk-like base of the fungus is separated from the upper region by an inner membrane. The fruit body turns pale brown as it ages, finally splitting open to release masses of brown spores.

Grey Puffball (*Bovista plumbea*) and its relatives are even more ball-shaped, lack a stalk region and are attached to the soil only tenuously. Initially white, the outer skin flakes off to reveal a grey parchment-like surface that later splits to release a purple-brown mass of spores.

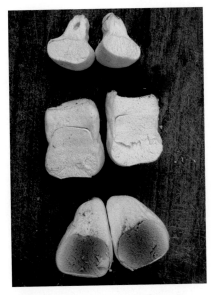

Meadow Puffball, showing the internal membrane.

How to cook puffballs

Small, firm puffballs can be cooked whole or sliced and fried like potatoes. Try poaching them in milk in the oven, seasoned with onion, salt and pepper, and served on a bed of spinach. Alternatively, dice and sauté puffball, onion, leek and celery before stewing with potato and chicken or vegetable stock. When soft, purée the mixture in a blender to produce a delicious, smooth-textured soup.

Puffballs ready for the pot.

4 Woodland edibles

This chapter starts with woodland puffballs, some of which grow on dead wood, others on the ground. These are followed by the best edibles to be found growing on the ground under trees. The latter part of the chapter deals with the edibles that grow on living or dead wood including tree stumps. It concludes with the truffles, a group of fungi that fruit underground.

Woodland puffballs

Woodland habitats are good hunting grounds for edible puffballs, but great care needs to be taken to ensure that what is collected really is a puffball.

Pestle Puffball ready to eat.

The gregarious Stump Puffball growing on dead wood.

There is no identification problem with the Pestle Puffball (*Handkea excipuliformis* or *Calvatia excipuliformis*), an occasional species found in soil near woodland edges and in parks. Initially pear-shaped, it expands to a height of 10–15cm to resemble a bulbous drumstick or pestle, with the stalk region making up 50–75 per cent of the total height. The old, leathery, brown stalk region may persist for several years.

Common Puffballs (*Lycoperdon perlatum*) frequent leaf and needle litter in woodland and occur on woodchip. About the size of a hen's egg, the upper region of the fruit body is initially covered with spiny warts and granules, but these soon fall off to leave a smooth ochre-white skin. The similar Stump Puffball (*Lycoperdon pyriforme*) is more pear-shaped and grows in dense clusters on tree stumps and rotting wood. It is rarely more than 3cm across but its lack of size is made up for by its gregarious habit. Try coating these puffballs in batter and deep-frying them.

All puffballs are edible, but there are a number of similar-shaped woodland fungi that range from inedible, through mildly poisonous to potentially fatal.

Puffball hunters need to acquaint themselves with the earthballs, which also grow in gardens and on tree-lined pavements. Smelling of rubber, the Common Earthball (*Scleroderma citrinum*) is the shape of a flattened golf ball, with a patterned surface of yellow-brown, crocodile-like markings. As with puffballs, the skin finally splits open to reveal a mass of powdery spores. Scaly Earthball (*Scleroderma verrucosum*) is more finely patterned, with small brown scales and a grooved, stem-like base.

When cut in half, earthballs reveal a thick skin (up to 5mm deep) in contrast to the thin-skinned puffballs. Very young earthballs are white inside but quickly mature to a purplish black, mottled with white. Earthballs have been used to adulterate truffles and to bulk up sausages, but they are mildly poisonous (causing nausea and stomach ache) and should not be eaten.

The egg stage of the Stinkhorn (*Phallus impudicus*; *see* page 73), identified by the jelly layer beneath its skin, is a harmless puffball lookalike. Also puffball-like but poisonous are the young stages of *Amanita* species (*see* page 181). If a sliced 'puffball' reveals a miniature 'mushroom' inside, do not eat it.

must know

Before you cook woodland puffballs, wipe them clean and then cut each one in half vertically. Unless the inside of the fungus is firm, white and of a uniform texture, surrounded by a skin no thicker than a fingernail, do not eat it.

Cep and other edible boletes

One fungal family, the Boletaceae, brings more joy to the dedicated mushroom hunter than most of the other fungi put together. Often known as the boletes, they share several common features.

They are mushroom-shaped with a cap and central stalk, but in place of gills on the cap underside is a spongy layer of vertically arranged tubes, from which the spores are discharged. The openings of these are known as pores, and in most species they are clearly visible to the naked eye.

Unlike the pore-bearing bracket fungi such as Chicken of the Woods (*see* page 170), the fruit body of a bolete is soft-textured and ephemeral, and it does not grow on wood. The layer of tubes in a bolete can also easily be separated from the overlying cap flesh. Boletes are mycorrhizal (*see* page 42), growing in association with tree roots. Many of the 100-plus species found in northern Europe grow only in association with one, or a limited number of, tree species. The different species of bolete vary greatly in size, cap colour and surface texture, pore shape

A collection of nine different species of bolete from a foray to broadleaved and coniferous woodland.

and colour, stem thickness, and overall colour and markings. Classifying them is not easy, and some experts have renamed certain species of *Boletus* as *Xerocomus*, which means that the same fungus has a different Latin name in different books.

Of all the boletes, the most highly prized is undoubtedly *Boletus edulis*, now known as Cep, from the French word *cèpe*, which refers to its tree-trunk-like stem. Its older English name of Penny Bun is more descriptive of the cap, while to the Americans it is the King Bolete, in German it is *Steinpilz*, meaning 'stone mushroom', and to the Italians they are *Funghi Porcini*, or 'piglet mushrooms'. The annual global trade in Ceps and related species – fresh, canned, dried or preserved in oil – runs into hundreds of tonnes. In Britain, fresh Ceps (not always local) are becoming more widely available and retail at up to £50 a kilogram. Specimens weighing 1–2kg are not unusual: Ceps can be large as well as solid.

The author as a young man with a collection of Ceps.

Depending on the weather, Ceps may occur between June and December but are most frequent in September and October, often appearing before many of the other woodland fungi. Look for them specifically under Oak or Beech trees, although they are also found with a range of different trees, including Birch, pine and Sweet Chestnut. Ceps are most frequent near woodland margins or in clearings, but they are often difficult to spot against a background of dead leaves. In Birch and pine woods, they often grow in close proximity to the more flamboyant red and white Fly Agaric, which thus provides a useful marker.

Brown spore print from a Cep.

A young Cep has an extraordinary shape, in that the diameter of its hemispherical cap is smaller than that of the stem base – rather like the shape of a champagne cork. The thick-fleshed cap initially has

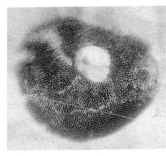

A mature Cep showing pale straw-coloured pores and a network on the stem.

must know

There are more than 20 species of *Boletus*. While many, like the Cep, are edible, some are poisonous if not well cooked and others cause severe gastric upset. To be safe, do not collect any bolete that has orange or red pores, and do not eat any in which the flesh discolours a vivid blue on cutting.

A Bitter Bolete, showing the brown network and pink spore deposit at the stem apex.

a white bloom; later it expands to reach 30cm across in diameter and flattens to a shallow convex shape. Generally smooth (rarely faintly wrinkled), the cap is slightly sticky when wet and ranges in colour from pale beige to red brown, always with a paler margin. The small round pores are initially white, ageing to straw-yellow and finally pale olive-green, but do not change colour on handling. The broad, stocky stem is noticeably swollen at its base and is covered by a raised white honeycomb network that is clearly visible just below the cap.

The prized firm, white cap flesh softens with age, when the tubes tend to become watery. Worse still, old Ceps are very prone to maggot infestation, especially in the stem, so check in the field and remember that small is often better.

The bolete group includes Devil's Bolete (*see* page 185) and the Lurid Bolete (*Boletus luridus*). Both are poisonous. The species most commonly confused with Cep is Bitter Bolete (*Tylopilus felleus*). While it is less robust than Cep, Bitter Bolete also has a brown cap and white pores when young, although these later turn pink (it has pink spores) and bruise brown with handling. The angular pores are larger than those of Cep, and the stem network is brown and visible all over the stem. As its name suggests, the flesh is extremely bitter, such that a single specimen in a collection of Ceps will render a whole dish unpalatable.

Do not despair if you can't find Ceps, as there are a number of other boletes whose culinary merits are almost as good. The best of these is Bay Bolete (*Boletus badius*), named after its shiny bay or chestnut-brown cap, which, unlike that of the Cep, is not paler at its margin. Typically less robust than the Cep, with a shallowly convex, less fleshy cap measuring up to 15cm across, Bay Bolete grows in a variety of woodland types but is most frequent in the autumn under conifers on acid soils. In moist weather the cap is slightly sticky, but when dry it is more velvety. The tubes close to the stem are often shorter than the others, resulting in a 'moat' around the stem. The angular, creamy-yellow pores turn olive coloured in older specimens,

How to cook Ceps

The caps are best sliced or cut into chunks prior to cooking, drying or pickling. I prefer to peel the stems, which usually have a firmer texture than the caps, before thinly slicing them. For many dishes it is worth using a mixture of cap and stem pieces.

Thin slices of cap and stem are easily dried and can subsequently be used in soups and stews. Dried Cep also makes a very tasty mushroom powder (see page 58), and portions of young Cep preserve well in olive oil.

Mushroom soup made with Ceps.

How to cook Bay Boletes

Purists may look on Bay Bolete as only second best to Cep, but it does have a big advantage over its relative in that middle-aged specimens are much less prone to maggot infestation. The stems of Bay Boletes are rather more fibrous, and I usually discard them if using fresh specimens, They can, however, be dried, along with the caps, for later use or for making into mushroom powder. If the tubes are a little mushy (never wash a bolete), they can easily be separated from the pale yellow flesh and discarded. Don't be put off by the fact that the flesh of the Bay Bolete blues faintly when cut, as it has a sweet, slightly fruity taste and can be used in a wide range of dishes.

Bay Bolete.

**Yellow-cracked
Bolete.**

and on touching they quickly turn blue-green, as if bruised. The pale brown cylindrical stem lacks the Cep's raised network but is covered with darker, longitudinal fibres.

Worthington Smith, a Victorian mushroom hunter who was perhaps rather less careful in his identification than his passion warranted, wrote, 'Before I properly knew *Boletus edulis*, I ate all sorts of boleti in mistake for it, notably *Boletus chrysenteron.*' Fortunately for Mr Smith, the Red-cracked Bolete (*Boletus chrysenteron*) is edible, as is Yellow-cracked Bolete (*Boletus subtomentosus*), although they are distinctly inferior to both the Cep and Bay Bolete. They are the commonest of the boletes and grow in mixed woodland, especially with Birch, as well as with garden trees and in city parks.

Typically measuring only 6–8cm across, both the Red-cracked and Yellow-cracked boletes have large, angular yellow pores that bruise faintly blue green (less so in the Yellow-cracked) and a pale brown cap that cracks to reveal the flesh colour beneath – this is red in *chrysenteron* and yellow in *subtomentosus*. The former has a yellow stem tinged with red, a colour not found on the latter's stem. The flesh of both species is much softer than that of the

Cep or Bay Bolete and lacks the distinctive taste, but if there is nothing better to hand they can be used in soups or stews.

Boletes with tiny scales on their stems are placed in the genus *Leccinum*. The commonest of these are associated with Birch trees and include Orange Birch Bolete (*Leccinum versipelle*), a large fungus that many consider to be an excellent edible species. It has the advantage of a long season, fruiting from June to December. When young, the domed, brick-red cap is hardly wider than the stocky stem, but it quickly expands to as much as 25cm across, when it fades to an orange brown. The felt-like cap skin overhangs at the margins. The tiny, round, pale grey pores turn brown with age and do not change colour with handling. The long, tapering white stem is covered with tiny brownish-black scales. This bolete is often swollen at its base, where young specimens bruise blue-green with handling.

Orange Birch Bolete can be used in cooking in place of Cep. Don't be alarmed when the cut flesh of both cap and stem turns a greyish violet and then black (especially noticeable when the fungi are cooked).

Orange Birch Bolete – note the orange cap and dark stem scales.

There are several other orange-capped boletes of a similar size to Orange Birch Bolete, but these grow with different tree species. One of these is the Orange Oak Bolete (*Leccinum quercinum*), a less common species of southern Oak woods. Apart from its habitat, it is characterised by a brick-red cap colour and russet-brown scales on its stem. It is another edible species whose pale flesh darkens when cut and on cooking.

Leccinum aurantiacum has an orange-red cap and pale grey pores that bruise brown. The brown scales are much denser towards the base of the stem. This edible species grows with poplars and the closely related Aspen tree.

The Orange Birch Bolete is not the only edible *Leccinum* species that grows with Birch trees. Of the others in this group, the commonest species is the Brown Birch Bolete (*Leccinum scabrum*), which often occurs in the same localities as its orange relative. It has a marginally smaller cap and stem diameter, but differs mostly in its colour. The slightly mottled cap is a dull brown, is slightly sticky in wet weather and lacks the overhanging margins. The stem base does not bruise blue-green. The pale grey pores bruise brown on handling, and the rather soft flesh shows little colour change on cutting and does not darken when cooked.

Many beginners assume that Brown Birch Boletes are just darker-coloured varieties of Orange Birch Boletes, observing only the cap colour difference and not the other features outlined above. Misidentification is not serious, more a cause for disappointment, as Brown Birch Bolete is far inferior to its orange relative as an edible species. The tubes quickly become waterlogged, which together with the soft flesh results in a rather soggy culinary experience. The cap flesh (discard the fibrous stems and waterlogged tubes) is only worth eating when the fruit bodies are still young and firm.

Another very common brown fungus that is similar in size to the Brown Birch Bolete and also

did you know?

Not all orange-capped boletes have scales on their stem. The very common Larch Bolete (*Suillus grevillei*) has a smooth stem and a bright orange, sticky cap. See page 124 for more details.

has a sticky cap is Brown Roll-rim (*Paxillus involutus*). It is often associated with Birch (and with other trees) as well and even has a comparable moist texture. As the name implies, it has an inrolled cap margin, but the cap bears brown, decurrent gills, not pores. Unusually, and in common with the boletes, the spore-producing tissue of the species is easily separated from the cap flesh.

Coniferous woodland can prove fruitful in the search for both Cep and Bay Bolete, but there are several other common edible boletes that are specifically associated with conifers. These differ from the other boletes in having a very glutinous (sticky) feel to the cap, and they are classified separately in the genus *Suillus*.

**Brown Roll-rim.
The gills bruise dark
brown when handled.**

Slippery Jack (*Suillus luteus*) is an autumn-fruiting species that grows in small groups under pines or other conifers. Unusually for a bolete, the immature tubes are covered by a white veil, parts of which remain on the stem as a floppy ring that darkens in older fruit bodies. The medium-sized, fleshy, chestnut to purple-brown, slimy cap expands to a diameter of 15cm. Its surface dries like varnish, often with moss and leaf litter fragments stuck to it. The small, rounded, lemon-yellow pores age a pale brown. The creamy-yellow lower part of the stem browns with age. Above the ring, the stem mirrors the pore colour but is dotted with small brown scales.

must know

The slimy cap covering of all *Suillus* species should be peeled or cut away and discarded before cooking. If possible, collect specimens during dry weather as this reduces the amount of slime.

The very pale yellow flesh of Slippery Jack is initially firm but quickly softens as the mushroom grows. It lacks the distinctive flavour of *Boletus* species but is good for pickling and dries well. In this form it is often sold in Europe as Pine Bolete.

Several related species that also grow with pine include Bovine Bolete (*Suillus bovinus*). This has a cap the colour of a Jersey cow and a surface texture that is more shiny than slimy. The stem lacks a ring and the large olive-yellow, angular pores are shallow and often subdivided. Bovine Bolete is worth eating only when it is very young as the flesh soon becomes maggot-ridden and develops a rubbery texture.

The very common and easily spotted sticky-capped Larch Bolete (*Suillus grevillei*) grows from the roots of Larch trees, fruiting from midsummer to early autumn. Neither European nor Japanese

Slippery Jack.

Bovine Bolete.

larches are native to Britain, but they are often found in parks and around the borders of coniferous plantations. The convex, bright orange-yellow viscous caps of Larch Bolete bear short tubes with yellow pores that bruise brown when handled, and the stem sports a sticky ring towards its apex. As with Slippery Jack, the slimy surface layer of this species should be removed before cooking. Larch Bolete is best used in soups and stews.

Larch Bolete.

The morels

Among dedicated mushroom hunters, the morels are so highly prized that they are placed second only to the truffles (*see* page 176). And as with truffles, those who know where to find morels keep such information a carefully guarded secret.

Morels are collected for both home consumption and export (mostly in their dried state) in Europe (especially Italy and France), Asia (India and Pakistan) and North America. In the American Midwest, the state of Minnesota even holds morel festivals and competitions, while local radio stations there report on the progress of the season.

Morels belong to a different group of fungi from the majority of species mentioned in this book – namely, the Ascomycetes. Their spores are produced inside elongated sac-like structures (*see* page 32) and are not dispersed from gills or pores. Of greater significance to the mushroom hunter is their spring fruiting season. In southern England, morels often appear as early as March; in the Midlands the season starts by mid-April;

Spring bounty – morels ready for cooking.

Close-up of the honeycomb-like cap region of a morel.

and further north morels are less common and fruit a little later. Most British finds are made after heavy rain between April and early June. With the exception of St George's Mushroom (*see* page 102), this is before the main mushroom season starts. Morels are now also being grown commercially.

In Britain, there are a number of different species of true morel, all of which bear a superficial resemblance to a brain or section of honeycomb on a stalk. Details such as cap colour, shape and architecture, together with the mode of attachment to the stem and the ratio of cap size to stem length, are all important for accurate identification. Confusingly, some morels have several common English names and different authors also cite different Latin names for the same species. However, what matters to the mushroom hunter is that they are all edible and excellent.

Common Morel (*Morchella esculenta*) has an egg-shaped (often asymmetrical), grey or yellow-brown, hollow cap that is 5–15cm tall. The cap is covered in an irregular pattern of pits resembling an untidy honeycomb, the pits being darker in colour than the edge walls. The cap base curls under, and fuses with, the top of the hollow, white, slightly furrowed, brittle stem. This is broader at its base and about the same length as the cap. The very similar *Morchella rotunda* has a larger, rounder, more fawn-coloured cap that is separated from the stem apex by a shallow groove.

A Black Morel, with its darker, elongated cap.

Black Morels are more narrowly conical in shape than Common Morels, with an elongated cap and regular pits set between vertical ribs that are nearly parallel to one another. They are typically a dark brown colour and include several closely related species: *Morchella elata*, *Morchella conica* and *Morchella costata*.

The Semifree Morel (*Mitrophora semilibera*) is similar to the Black Morel but has a much longer, mealy stem that is attached halfway up the undersurface of the small, pointed cap. Also edible, it occurs on damp base-rich (alkaline) soil in woods, gardens and wet meadows in late spring, often in association with the yellow-flowered Lesser Celandine.

How to cook morels

All morels have a mild, pleasant smell when fresh. Clean the stem bases before transporting the fungi to prevent soil from entering the cap pits. Cut each one vertically, removing any hidden insects or dirt from the pits or hollow stem, and check that the hollow stem and cap are single-chambered (*see* 'watch out!' box opposite).

Do not eat raw or partially cooked morels as they can contain poisonous hydrazines, which cause nausea, vomiting and abdominal pain. A prolonged, gentle cooking not only volatises the hydrazines but also enhances the wonderful flavour of the fungi.

To be on the safe side with morels, it is a good idea to blanch them before cooking. Use only firm, dry and sweet-smelling specimens, not those that have started to rot. Try slicing them horizontally before cooking, as this results in very attractive shapes. Whole or half morels can also be stuffed and baked with breadcrumbs, Parmesan cheese and chopped parsley, and the fungi go well with a sauce made of cream or yogurt and a little wine. Their wonderful meaty flavour will equally transform any soup or stew.

Morels are easily dried (*see* page 58), when they turn black, shrink by at least 60 per cent and lose any volatile hydrazines that may have been present. They can be readily reconstituted by soaking in warm water (or wine) for 20 minutes, when their size and texture is little different from fresh specimens. Some imported morels are dried over open fires, which results in an interesting smoky flavour.

Semifree Morels showing the long stem attached halfway up the cap and the single chamber inside the cap and stem.

The False Morel, or Turban Fungus (*Gyromitra esculenta*), is a dangerous morel lookalike despite its Latin specific epithet, which means 'edible'. It also fruits in the early spring, often starting three or four weeks earlier than the true morels, and is a rare fungus of coniferous woods. The fist-sized, chestnut-brown cap has folds rather than pits, and the stem and cap are multi-chambered rather than having a single hollow like the true morels. It contains gyromitrin which is metabolised in the stomach to monomethylhydrazine, a chemical that has been used as a rocket fuel and is the probable cause of fatalities following ingestion of the fungus. In short, do not eat it.

The poisonous False Morel – note that the cap consists of deep folds, in contrast to the honeycomb pits of the true morels.

Chanterelle

Chanterelle (*Cantharellus cibarius*) is definitely among the top five best edibles for Europe's mushroom hunters. Its rich egg-yolk colour (not lost in cooking) is coupled with a firm flesh that has a whiff of apricots and a flavour imbued with subtle aftertastes.

must know

There are some other woodland fungi of similar appearance to Chanterelles when viewed from above. However, these lookalikes have true gills (or spines, as in Wood Hedgehog; *see* page 132), and either a white spore print (as with Common Yellow Russula; *see* page 139) or rusty-brown spores (as with species of *Cortinarius*; *see* page 184).

The relatively small size of each funnel-shaped fruit body (2–10cm across) is compensated for by the fact that Chanterelles are highly sociable, so search carefully among fallen leaves and vegetation in the area of any initial find and you may discover more.

Under the cap, in place of gills, Chanterelles have blunt-edged, deep wrinkles that radiate and fork like fan vaulting from the chunky, tapered stem. They produce a creamy-yellow spore print.

Cantharellus cibarius is most common among moss under Beech or mixed broad-leaved trees where

Chanterelles in moss.

Trumpet Chanterelle (*Cantharellus tubaeformis*) has a brown cap and a longer stem. It is edible but has a sharper flavour than Chanterelle.

the ground is sloping. Old woodland on a moist, steep slope above a river is an ideal hunting ground. They also grow under conifers, especially in Wales and Scotland. Look for them at any time from May through to late autumn.

False Chanterelle (*Hygrophoropsis aurantiaca*) is frequently mistaken for the real thing; fortunately for most people, the result is disappointing but innocuous. For a minority, however, the mistake is less pleasant, as the species can cause gastric upset and even unpleasant hallucinations. False Chanterelle is much more common than Chanterelle under conifers and on heathland. It also has a darker orange colour, with crowded, true gills, an initially inrolled cap margin and a less substantial stem.

False Chanterelle – note the crowded gills.

Wood Hedgehog

On occasions when I have been on the lookout for late-fruiting Chanterelles, I have come across the Wood Hedgehog (*Hydnum repandum*) instead. This is never a disappointment, as this species is every bit as good as Chanterelle.

Wood Hedgehog, like Chanterelle, is a fungus of broad-leaved woodland, especially among moss in Beech woods, although it also grows under conifers. Look for it in late summer and early autumn. It is gregarious, occasionally growing in rings, and neighbouring caps often fuse. The fleshy, wavy-edged cap is frequently of an irregular shape and varies from off-white, through cream to yellow-orange, when it looks very like Chanterelle if viewed from above.

The big surprise comes when the Wood Hedgehog is turned over; in place of gills or the Chanterelle's wrinkles is a mass of brittle, vertical spines – hence its common English name. The spines occasionally run down onto the paler, short, stout, solid stem, which is often misshapen and attached to the cap towards one side like a hoof – hence its common French name of *Pied de Mouton* (meaning 'sheep's foot').

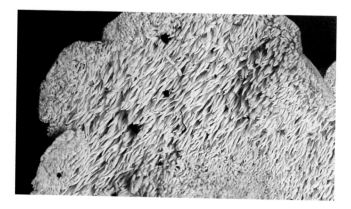

Close-up of a Wood Hedgehog.

Wood Hedgehogs in a basket.

Smaller, more russet-brown specimens of Wood Hedgehog, with flatter caps and thinner, centrally placed hollow stems, are considered by many mycologists to be a separate species (*Hydnum rufescens*); others class it as a variety of *H. repandum*. To the mushroom hunter this is largely irrelevant, as both of these so-called 'tooth fungi' are edible. Other tooth fungi include a delicate species that grows from pine cones and a few rarer ones with grey or brown zoned caps. None of these is poisonous, so Wood Hedgehog is a safe mushroom for beginners.

How to cook Wood Hedgehogs

If possible, cut or brush off any dirt from the stem bases of Wood Hedgehogs before putting them in your collecting basket. This negates the job of removing soil from between the spines with the point of a knife later on. Some fussy French chefs discard the spines, but this is necessary only on older specimens, when they can taste rather bitter.

Any bitterness in the fungi (some sources claim that *H. rufescens* is more bitter than *H. repandum*) is removed on cooking, especially when the mushrooms are blanched first. Because they have thick flesh they can be successfully pickled or even frozen, preferably after blanching.

Horn of Plenty

Here is a mushroom with a range of names that reflect the ambiguity of attitudes to its edibility and appearance. In Britain, it is known as both the Horn of Plenty and Trumpet of Death, and similar pairs of names are found in France, Spain and Italy.

must know

Horn of Plenty is a difficult mushroom to spot and is easily mistaken for a withered leaf. If you do find one, it is worth getting on all fours to look for more, as they usually grow in troops.

Several Horns of Plenty well hidden among dead leaves.

The artistic cornucopian emblem, overflowing with flowers, fruit and corn, contrasts with the more macabre picture of the fungi representing trumpets being blown by dead bodies beneath the soil.

Horn of Plenty (*Craterellus cornucopioides*) is an autumn-fruiting fungus and grows among moss and leaf litter under broad-leaved trees, most frequently on acid soil under Beech. The funnel-shaped cap (rarely more than 10cm high and 6–8cm across) is hollow down to the base of its stem. The wavy, split

top edge of the 'horn' is rolled under like the end of a trumpet. Its grey-brown outer surface bears a frosty bloom and lacks gills, although it may be marked with longitudinal wrinkles. The inner surface is a dingy brown or black. The only lookalike is Ashen Chanterelle (*C. cinereus*); also edible, this has a network of gill-like wrinkles on its underside.

Horn of Plenty has not always received a rapturous response in Britain – one Victorian author wrote of his surprise when he read in a 'foreign book' that the species was edible. He added, 'Up to then we should have thought as much of stewing our slippers.' The fungus does have a rather leathery texture, reminiscent of the famous scene in the film *The Gold Rush*, in which Charlie Chaplin cooks and eats his boot. It is, however, the pleasant aroma and strong flavour of Horn of Plenty that makes it a popular ingredient with restaurateurs.

Discard any old specimens, which will be black, flaccid and emitting a foetid odour. The others will require careful cleaning; this is achieved by slicing them in half lengthways and removing any dirt or animal life from the stem base.

Ashen Chanterelle.

The russulas

Two important groups of fungus that grow on the ground in woodlands are the russulas, or brittle gills (*Russula* spp.), and the milk caps (*Lactarius* spp.). They are all mycorrhizal (*see* page 42) with tree roots, and most have medium or large fleshy fruit bodies.

Their anatomy differs from all other mushrooms, resulting in a brittle, friable texture. The cylindrical stems are without a ring and are easily snapped like blackboard chalk, while the gills and cap flesh can be crumbled like Cheshire cheese. Many of these fungi form a relationship with just one or a small number of tree species, including most of our native species (but not Maple or Ash) and some introduced species (including many conifers but not Sycamore).

There are over 140 British species of *Russula*. Unlike the milk caps (*see* pages 140–145), they do not exude latex and most species lack intermediate gills (though the gills may fork near the cap margin), giving the cap underside a very neat appearance. Many russulas have brightly coloured caps.

Four different species of *Russula*.

watch out!

When collecting woodland fungi, always check that there is no cup-like volva at the stem base. The volva is a feature of species of *Amanita*, several of which are poisonous (*see* page 181).

Charcoal Burner.

Russula spore colour (and gill colour, with a few exceptions) is white, cream or pale yellow. Because many russulas are similar in appearance, accurate identification to species level may require chemical tests or microscopic examination of the spores. However, no russulas are seriously poisonous if well cooked, although many are described by British authors as inedible or 'edible but not worthwhile'. This is partly because of their rather al dente texture and the fact that slugs, snails and maggots usually get to them first. Some species have an acrid taste and a few are mildly poisonous (especially if eaten raw), but many are eaten and pickled in Eastern Europe. A woodland foray between May and November is always likely to turn up some edible russulas.

One of the most common russulas of broad-leaved woodland (especially where Beech is present) is *Russula cyanoxantha*, known as the Peacock Russule or Rainbow Russule in Victorian times, but now usually referred to as the Charcoal Burner, a translation of *Charbonnier*, the French name for the species. The firm, slightly greasy cap is initially deeply convex, later flattening and expanding to reach up to 15cm in diameter. It is very variable in colour, although usually lilac grey with patches of green, blue and yellow, like a peacock's tail or the multicoloured flame seen when charcoal is burnt. The crowded, white, forked gills are unusually pliable for a russula. It has little smell and a mild, nutty taste, and it is best sliced and fried, although it also pickles well.

There are a number of green-coloured russulas, including a variety of the Charcoal Burner and also the Grass Green Russula

An old (*left*) and young (*right*) Blackening Russula.

(*Russula aeruginea*), which has buff-yellow gills and grows on damp ground under Birch. The latter fungus is best left alone as it can cause digestive upset. Less common and typically found with Beech or Oak is the Green-cracking Russula (*R. virescens*), deemed the tastiest of all the russulas. It is recognised by its dry, pale to mid-green cap, which has a scaly appearance as a result of marginal cracks that reveal the underlying white flesh. Its taste is comparable to that of hazelnuts and it has a firm texture. *Check* page 181 for features of the very poisonous Death Cap, as this also has an olive-green cap and so could possibly be confused with *R. virescens*.

With a chunky cap measuring up to 20cm across, Blackening Russula (*Russula nigricans*) is common in both broad-leaved and coniferous woods. Its cap is convex and creamy white when young, becoming funnel-shaped and soon turning brown and finally black. Atypically for a russula, its thick, distant gills include some of differing lengths, and old fruit bodies remain intact for many months. Older Blackening Russulas are tough and invariably maggot-ridden, but immature fruit bodies are worth eating. The white flesh has a fruity aroma and a mild, sweet taste, and stains rose-red and finally greyish black when cut.

did you know?

Aside from Blackening Russula, the only other common black mushroom is the edible Horn of Plenty (*see* page 134), but this is much smaller and does not have gills.

There are several yellow-capped species of russula, including Common Yellow Russula (*Russula ochroleuca*), which is a very frequent fungus of damp ground beneath trees. Its ochre-yellow cap has a faintly grooved margin and bears moderately crowded, creamy-white adnate gills, which, like the white stem, may turn grey with age. Common Yellow Russula has a white spore print, and is mild in flavour when young but more peppery with age.

Golden Russula (*Russula risigallina* or *R. lutea*) grows under broad-leaved trees and differs from Common Yellow Russula in having an apricot-yellow cap, deep-yellow gills that produce an ochre-yellow spore print, and a mild-tasting flesh that smells faintly of apricots. The stem stays white.

Avoid the inedible Geranium-scented Russula (*Russula fellea*), a late-autumn species found under Beech. The cap, gills and stem of this species are all yellowish brown in colour, but the *Pelargonium*-smelling flesh has a very hot taste.

My favourite among the yellow-capped russulas is the Yellow Swamp Russula (*Russula claroflava*), which fruits from midsummer among moss on wet ground under Birch or Alder. It has a slightly sticky, buttercup-yellow cap, creamy-yellow gills and fruity-smelling, mild-tasting flesh.

The pinky-red Bare-toothed Russula (*Russula vesca*) has a skin that retracts from the cap margin, exposing white gill ends. It is another russula that is good to eat.

Yellow Swamp Russula.

> **watch out!**
>
> Beware the red-capped Beechwood Sickener (*Russula nobilis* or *R. mairei*) and the similar Sickener (*R. emetica*; *see* photograph on page 180), which grows under conifers. Both of these species can cause vomiting if eaten.

Saffron Milk Cap

Milk caps are related to russulas (*see* page 136) and also have unusually brittle fruit bodies, but they are distinguished from the latter in that they release a 'latex' when their flesh or gills are damaged. This liquid is usually milky white or watery, and is often acrid, rendering most milk caps inedible or mildly poisonous. Many species have decurrent gills at maturity, and unlike the colourful russulas most are white or brown.

A milk cap exuding milky-white latex from its scratched gills.

A very visible exception to this is the brightly coloured Saffron Milk Cap (*Lactarius deliciosus*), which exudes a carrot-coloured latex. Reputed to be the fungus mentioned as a good edible by the Roman writer Pliny, and possibly represented in a fresco at Pompeii, it is also a firm favourite in Poland, Russia and North America. Given this endorsement and such an unambiguous Latin name, it is surprising to find that there is considerable disagreement in Britain over its edible properties. As we shall see, this may be due to the fact (overlooked in many books) that there are several very similar-looking species that vary in both

Saffron Milk Caps in grass under pines.

Saffron Milk Caps, showing patches of green and the pits at their stem bases.

taste and texture. Accurate identification here is not so much a matter of life or death as of the quality of the ensuing meal.

The true Saffron Milk Cap is restricted to pine woods (both our native Scots Pine and introduced species) on acidic or sandy soil. Initially domed and with an inrolled wavy or lobed margin, the cap expands to a diameter of 20cm and becomes funnel-shaped; flat on top, or with a slight central depression. It is also moist and sticky when young, later becoming dry, hoary, and exhibiting concentric rings of dark orange on a background of reddish orange. The orange colour fades on older caps, which often develop green patches, especially after handling.

When cut, the moderately crowded, arching, saffron-coloured gills exude a bright orange, mild-tasting (or very slightly bitter) latex. This latex dries green and, along with the cap and stem, the gills of older specimens also develop green patches. The short, broad, pale orange, hollow stem is often partially buried among discarded pine needles. The lower half is dotted with deep-orange pit-like depressions. When cut, the pale yellow, sweet-smelling flesh of both the stem and cap rapidly turns orange and then slowly green.

must know

Look for Saffron Milk Caps under pine trees from midsummer to late autumn. It is more common in Scotland, Northern Ireland and parts of Wales. The presence of the carrot-coloured pits near the stem base is a key feature that separates *Lactarius deliciosus* from other closely related species.

False Saffron Milk Caps growing under spruce. Note the absence of stem pits.

How to cook Saffron Milk Caps

Apart from mistaken identity (*see* below), two reasons for the disappointing culinary reports about Saffron Milk Cap are that they may taste bitter and the stems can be tough. This is easily rectified by rejecting the stems and blanching the caps to reduce any bitterness. Both the unusual crunchy texture and the wonderful colour are maintained by brushing the caps with oil and cooking them briefly under a pre-heated grill.

Saffron Milk Caps can also be oven-baked, they make a colourful garnish for fish dishes and they go well with pasta. Small pieces may be pickled in oil (when the colour is largely preserved) or brine, but they do not dry well. As with eating beetroot, one outcome of ingesting Saffron Milk Caps may be a darkening of the urine; don't be alarmed, however, as this is not a long-term side effect.

Saffron Milk Cap grows in groups, so quantity is not so much of a problem as quality; older fruit bodies are invariably full of maggots. Always go for young ones and check for squatters before carting them home.

False Saffron Milk Cap (*Lactarius deterrimus*) is very similar to *L. deliciosus* but always grows with spruce (*Picea* spp.) and smells

of carrots. Its slightly smaller, only faintly banded orange cap turns green after frost. Its stem base is devoid of orange pits and the orange milk turns purplish red before fading to green. The rarer *L. salmonicolor* grows under spruce and firs (*Abies* spp.), although it lacks concentric zones on the cap and any green discoloration. Both species are frequently mistaken for Saffron Milk Cap, but their resinous, bitter flavour is decidedly inferior. *L. sanguifluus*, a species from southern Europe (it is not found in Britain), is very similar again. It bleeds a blood-red latex, is even tastier than *L. deliciosus* and is another strong contender for the fungus depicted on the Pompeii fresco (*see* page 140).

Another Saffron Milk Cap lookalike is the Fenugreek Milk Cap (*Lactarius helvus*). It is found on peaty soil with pine or Birch, and has a slightly scaly, russet-pink, non-banded cap and a watery, acrid latex that smells of celery or fenugreek. Woolly Milk Cap (*L. torminosus*; *see* page 44) also grows with Birch (although not with conifers), and its flesh-coloured cap is marked with darker rings and has a fleecy, inrolled margin. The pink gills exude an extremely bitter, white latex. Both *L. helvus* and *L. torminosus* are poisonous if eaten raw or without careful preparation, so steer clear of them.

Other edible milk caps

Saffron Milk Cap (*see* page 140) receives a mixed press in Britain over its edible qualities and many fungus guides ignore other species of *Lactarius* altogether. However, many of these can be eaten after careful preparation without apparent ill effect.

The chemicals responsible for the acrid taste sometimes found in milk caps are known as sesquiterpenes, and when acrid milk caps are eaten raw or without adequate cooking these chemicals may irritate the intestinal tract, causing pain, sickness and diarrhoea. Proper cooking, drying or pickling negates these effects, and the fungi can then be used sparingly in cooking like pepper and other spices. The identification of some species of *Lactarius* is confirmed by tasting a tiny drop of the latex, although be prepared to spit if you get a hot one! All edible milk caps, including those with orange latex, should be parboiled in water (change the water several times) before being cooked or preserved.

One of the largest of the acrid milk caps is the Peppery Milk Cap (*Lactarius piperatus*). This common autumn species is found in broad-leaved woodland (especially with Beech and Oak), where the creamy-white funnel-shaped caps grow to 15cm across. The

Peppery Milk Cap.

very crowded, often forked, creamy-yellow decurrent gills exude a white peppery milk. After parboiling, Peppery Milk Cap can be fried and eaten, but it is not good in stews. In Poland and Russia, the fungus is preserved in salt or vinegar, when the flesh stains greyish green.

Some species of *Lactarius* are identified by their unusual aroma. Coconut-scented Milk Cap (*L. glyciosmus*) is found on acid soil under Birch trees.

Coconut-scented
Milk Cap.

This small mushroom has pink tints to its grey-brown cap, which is shaped like a shallow funnel with a small bump in the middle. Only a sparse amount of white latex is produced by damaged gills, and although this initially tastes mild, it becomes hotter after a minute. The smell is like that of desiccated coconut, and the fungus is considered more of a fun addition to a meal than a good edible species.

The Curry-scented Milk Cap (*L. camphoratus*) and Rufous Milk Cap (*L. rufus*) can be used as hot-tasting spices when dried and ground to a powder. They both grow in coniferous woods, and *L. camphoratus* is also found with Birch.

Rufous Milk Cap.

The Miller

The Miller (*Clitopilus prunulus*) is an excellent edible mushroom that can be readily identified with the use of three different senses.

The most obvious feature is its strong smell, variously described as like that of freshly milled flour, damp meal or bread dough. In addition to its unusual odour, the Miller has a strange texture to its cap surface. Many books describe it as having the feel of kid-leather gloves – in other words, a soft, felty, matt surface that may become slightly sticky in damp weather. The most important visual features are the quite crowded, deeply decurrent gills, which produce a salmon-pink spore print.

The Miller is small to medium in size, usually measuring less than 10cm across, and has a creamy-white or dingy-beige cap and stem. Initially convex and with an inrolled margin, the thick-fleshed cap rapidly becomes funnel-shaped, usually with a central depression and irregular, undulating edge. The longer gills, which run down onto the stem, are interspersed with much shorter ones. The gills are initially white, turning flesh-pink as

good to know

The other common edible species that smells strongly of meal is St George's Mushroom (*see* page 102). This much larger, chunkier mushroom does not have decurrent gills and produces white spores. It fruits from April to June, some months before The Miller.

The Miller – note the flesh-coloured, decurrent gills.

the mushroom matures. The solid stem has a cottony base and is often slightly eccentric.

Look out for The Miller from midsummer to early November. It is associated with both broad-leaved and coniferous trees, and grows on rich soil, most frequently in rides and grassy clearings in woodland. It is also found in parkland and with heathers and Bilberry. Usually just two or three individuals grow together, although occasionally it produces rings.

watch out!

There are two superficially similar poisonous species that may occur in the same season and in the same habitat as The Miller: the Sweating Mushroom (also known as Fool's Funnel) and Livid Pinkgill (*see* page 186 for details of all of these). The first one produces a white spore print, which is the best way of distinguishing it from The Miller. Livid Pinkgill, meanwhile, also smells mealy when young and has pink spores, but it is generally much larger than The Miller and its yellow gills are sinuate, never decurrent.

The Sweating Mushroom, a poisonous Miller lookalike with white spores.

The deceivers

The Deceiver (*Laccaria laccata*) is one of the commonest of all woodland fungi in Britain, but as its name suggests it is also the species that causes the most identification problems for beginners.

The deception is twofold: first, both the overall size and relative proportion of cap to stem size vary enormously between individuals; and second, as the cap dries its colour and texture changes.

Deceivers are found from summer to late autumn, usually in large numbers among the leaf litter of broad-leaved woods, especially with Birch on acid soils. The small cap (1–4cm in diameter) soon flattens and may develop a central depression. When moist, the tawny to red-brown cap has a scurfy centre and finely grooved margin. Dried specimens lack the grooves and fade to a pale beige colour. The widely spaced, thick gills are flesh-brown in colour and produce a white spore print. The thin, fibrous stem is very variable in length and is often twisted and flattened.

Deceivers, showing flesh-coloured distant gills and short intermediate gills.

White spore print of The Deceiver.

Amethyst Deceivers growing in leaf litter.

How to cook deceivers

Although small, both The Deceiver and Amethyst Deceiver grow in troops and so can be collected in quantity. Discard the tough stems in all but very young specimens. Both species have a mild flavour and are best used in soups or, as they have a firm texture, in stews. If possible, try to use them alongside more highly flavoured species. Amethyst Deceiver keeps its colour so long as it is not overcooked, and can be used on pizzas or as a garnish for chicken or fish dishes. Both species can be dried, but try preserving Amethyst Deceivers in olive oil or a clear spirit, as the jars make great presents.

Growing in the same places as The Deceiver but with a preference for Beech leaf litter is Amethyst Deceiver (*Laccaria amethystina* or *L. amethystea*). This slightly larger fungus is easy to spot when young and moist, as the cap, gills and stem are a bright violet purple, although all later fade to a pale buff. Other features are as for The Deceiver.

Amethyst Deceiver may potentially be confused with the poisonous Lilac Bell Cap (*Mycena pura*). However, the latter is a much paler colour, smells of radish and has pinky-grey gills. Another poisonous woodland dweller is the Lilac Inocybe (*Inocybe geophylla* var. *lilacina*), which has a more conical cap, brown gills and a brown spore print.

Clouded Agaric

One of the largest of our woodland toadstools is the Clouded Agaric (*Clitocybe nebularis*), which produces troops or fairy rings among both broad-leaved and coniferous leaf and needle litter from late autumn through to Christmas.

How to cook Clouded Agarics

Clouded Agaric is not to everyone's taste and should not be consumed in large quantities. Use only the smaller, firm caps and discard the tough stems. Parboil the caps first, then cook them slowly over a low heat. The firm caps also pickle well in either brine or oil. Some people find Clouded Agaric difficult to digest and in others it produces transient rashes or headaches, so this is not a species to serve at a dinner party.

Initially deeply domed and with a very obviously inrolled margin, its cap matures to a flat funnel shape measuring up to 20cm in diameter. The mouse-grey to grey-brown cap colour is usually darker in the centre, and is obscured, or clouded, on young caps by a powdery white bloom. The very crowded, creamy-white gills become weakly decurrent with age and arch onto the creamy-grey, bulbous-based stem. Clouded Agaric has a strong smell that is variously described as mealy, aromatic or turnip-like. This puts some people off the idea of eating it.

must know

There are a number of smaller related species, including the Club-footed Funnel Cap (*Ampulloclitocybe clavipes*). This fungus has pale yellow gills, and like the Common Ink Cap (*see* page 95) it must not be consumed with alcohol.

Clouded Agaric.

Aniseed Toadstool

The combination of two unusual features – a blue cap and a smell of aniseed – make the Blue-green Funnel Cap, or Aniseed Toadstool (*Clitocybe odora*), easy to identify. A few other fungi are a similar colour and a number of species smell of aniseed, but this is our only aniseed-smelling blue mushroom!

The colour of book illustrations and photographs of this species differs widely as a result of variation between individuals of the species, artistic licence and poor print quality. The young cap colour is actually bluish green (best described as the colour of the label on a Heinz baked bean tin), but with age it fades to greyish green and finally creamy white. Initially convex, the cap matures flatter save for a central bump and is rarely more than 6cm across. The pale stem is flushed with a similar blue-green colour, as are the crowded, weakly decurrent gills, which produce white spores.

Aniseed Toadstool is an occasional species, fruiting from August to late autumn, usually among leaf litter under trees. It is most frequent with Beech or Oak, especially on calcium-rich soil. Used fresh or as a dried powder, it has an aniseed taste that enhances more mild-flavoured mushrooms and is especially good as an accompaniment to fish.

Verdigris Toadstool.

Aniseed Toadstool.

Orange Peel Fungus

The majority of wild mushrooms are collected for their flavour or texture, but only rarely do they add colour to a meal. Here is a fungus that does not score highly for its texture or taste, but it certainly adds colour and it is safe to eat raw or only lightly cooked.

watch out!

Because some fungi contain thermolabile toxins, mushroom hunters are advised to cook their finds before eating them.

Orange Peel Fungus (*Aleuria aurantia*) is a distant relative of the morels, and on account of its shape it is included in the group known as the cup fungi (*see* page 33). Many of these are small, brown and easily overlooked, but by contrast, the individual fruit bodies of Orange Peel Fungus can grow to 10cm across and often occur in large groups of tightly packed clusters. The shape, size and, most noticeably, the colour of *A. aurantia* is very similar to a discarded portion of orange peel, even down to the detail of the lower surface in young specimens, which is a paler colour and slightly downy.

must know

Be careful not to collect Orange Peel Fungus from tracks or other areas frequented by dog walkers.

Close-up of Orange Peel Fungus.

Scarlet Elf Cup (*Sarcoscypha coccinea*) fruits through the winter and early spring. It is less common than Orange Peel Fungus and grows on or under Hazel. The flesh is tougher than that of Orange Peel and it contains chemicals that destroy red blood cells; although these chemicals are detoxified by cooking, it is not worth taking the risk – instead, leave it and enjoy it for its beauty alone.

must know

The much smaller, disc-like Eyelash Fungus (*Scutellinia scutellata*) is a similar colour to Orange Peel Fungus and also grows on bare soil, although it is more common on rotting wood. It is not worth eating owing to its small size and the hairy margin of its fruit bodies.

Initially like a tiny cup with an inrolled margin, the fruit body, which lacks a stem, expands to become more saucer-shaped. As it matures, its shape becomes less regular and the wavy margin often splits to produce a lobed appearance. The thin flesh is easily broken.

Search for Orange Peel Fungus from late summer all the way through until Christmas. It grows on damp soil and occasionally among gravel, and is mostly found on and by woodland track edges, often in wheel ruts or perimeter ditches, but also among plants at woodland margins and on garden paths.

How to cook Orange Peel Fungus

Carefully wipe the fungi and cut off the points of attachment from their undersides. Larger specimens can be sliced into strips and eaten raw in salads or added to stir-fries. Smaller ones can be lightly stewed with the addition of sugar, and then added to fruit salads or served with hot jam or a fruit sauce. Pieces of the fungus can also be used to decorate the top of jellies or trifles. In France, they are eaten raw after being sprinkled with sugar and a little kirsch. Despite their bland flavour, they will provide a talking point at any dinner party.

Fawn Pluteus

In dry seasons rotting logs, old tree stumps and sawdust piles still manage to maintain a high moisture content. Many fungus species that grow on these substrates are inedible or even poisonous.

must know

Fawn Pluteus grows singly, or in small groups, on well-decayed wood. To confirm that you have identified it correctly you should make a spore print. The only medium-large fungi growing on wood that have a salmon-pink spore print are species of *Pluteus* and the related *Volvariella*. The latter (also edible) are much fleshier and the stem emerges from a bag-like volva.

The Honey Fungus (*see* page 156) is an exception but is difficult to identify and generally available only during the autumn. Fawn Pluteus (*Pluteus cervinus*) is also an exception, is easily identified and digested, and has a very long fruiting season from April to December.

The initially domed, moist cap of Fawn Pluteus soon flattens save for a central hump. It is typically 4–12cm across but larger when growing on sawdust. The colour varies from greyish brown to dark brown, with a few minute dark scales at the centre from

Fawn Pluteus growing on a rotting stump. Note the flesh-coloured free gills.

How to cook Fawn Pluteus

Many books on edible mushrooms state that *Pluteus cervinus* has little culinary value owing to its sharp taste and maggot-infested flesh. Notwithstanding such comments, I enjoy its tender flesh and unusual flavour. Over the last ten years I have regularly included Fawn Pluteus in the fry-ups that form part of my mushroom courses, and it always receives rave reviews.

The problem of maggots can be avoided by choosing only young specimens. Those collected in spring and early winter have the richest flavour and are normally free of maggots, as there are fewer insects around during these cooler seasons.

While the stems are usually too tough to be worth eating, the caps have thick, soft white flesh. This benefits from a brief, hot grilling, which imparts a crisper texture. Fawn Pluteus also mixes well with other edible species in soups and casseroles.

must know

The genus *Pluteus* includes a number of less common, slightly smaller wood-rotting species, all with free gills, pink spores and no ring. These include the edible Velvet *Pluteus* (*Pluteus umbrosus*), which has a cap covered in an irregular network of dark brown velvet scales. The only species of *Pluteus* that should be avoided is Willow Pluteus (*Pluteus salicinus*). This species has a grey-green cap and a blue-green flush to its stem base, similar to that of the Magic Mushroom (*see* page 70), and is reputed to contain the same psychoactive drug, psilocybin.

Velvet Pluteus.

where darker streaks radiate to the margin. The cap has the appearance of an animal hide – hence the word fawn in its common name – and its thick, soft, white flesh has a faint smell of radishes. The very crowded gills are obviously free of the stem; they start white but mature to a flesh-pink. Most unusually for a wood-rotting species, the fungus has a pink spore print. The tough, pale stem is patterned at its base with darker, longitudinal fibres and has neither a ring nor a volva.

Honey Fungus

Honey Fungus (*Armillaria mellea*) is one of the commonest and most variable of the wood-rotting fungi. It grows in both coniferous and broad-leaved woods, as well as in gardens. Genetic analysis and microscopic study has shown that Honey Fungus is actually a collective name for half a dozen closely related species, thus explaining its apparent variability.

A tuft of Honey Fungus on fallen wood.

The fungus has the reputation of being a serious parasite, killing trees and shrubs prior to living on the dead wood. In gardens, fruit trees and hedges of Privet and Leyland Cypress are particularly vulnerable; it even kills the Monkey Puzzle. Not all species are virulently parasitic – and they also live on dead wood and roots. More importantly for the mushroom hunter, they are all edible.

Because of the variability of Honey Fungus, novice collectors often have trouble when it comes to identifying members of the complex. Many characteristics also differ

Creamy-white spore print of Honey Fungus.

between young and mature specimens. The key features to look out for are listed below:

▶ **Habitat and habit**. Usually occurs in dense tufts, most commonly on tree stumps and fallen timber, but also on living trunks. When growing from roots or buried timber, the connection with wood may not be obvious – clumps can appear in the middle of a lawn.
▶ **Size**. There is wide variation in the ratio of cap width to stem length. Mature caps are 5–20cm in diameter and stems extend to 15cm high.
▶ **Colour**. Like honey, the cap and stem colour varies from yellowish, through olive to reddish brown. The central area of the young, deeply convex cap is usually speckled with darker scales (*see* photograph), but as the cap expands and flattens, these become less obvious. Older caps may develop a grooved margin and turn dark brown after frost.
▶ **Veil**. The young gills are covered by a cottony white or yellow veil, which later becomes the ring, although this is absent from one of the species (*A. tabescens*).
▶ **Gills**. The creamy-white or flesh-coloured gills develop brown flecks and arch up from the stem in older specimens.
▶ **Spores**. Look for a creamy-white spore deposit on bark, moss or the lowermost caps in a cluster.
▶ **Stem**. The fibrous stems are either cylindrical or swollen at the yellow-brown base and may be scaly below the ring.
▶ **Rhizomorphs**. Look for flattened, root-like, black 'bootlaces' – Honey Fungus uses these rhizomorphs to colonise new hosts.

Honey Fungus is an autumn species that continues well into December. In some years it fruits in profusion and very large numbers can be collected. Only the youngest specimens should be gathered, however, as older ones (which have an unpleasant smell) are tough, difficult to digest and may cause digestive upset.

watch out!

Some people find even well-cooked Honey Fungi difficult to digest and may suffer from a minor stomach upset after eating them. If you are trying them for the first time, eat only small amounts. Dark Honey Fungus (*Armillaria ostoyae*), which has a brown cap, stem base and scales on the underside of its ring, is most likely to cause these problems.

How to cook Honey Fungus

Honey Fungus contains thermolabile toxins and so should not be eaten raw. Blanch the caps for at least five minutes (discard the water afterwards) to remove the toxins, before dicing and cooking them in butter or adding them to soups or stews. The slightly bitter, rich, spicy flavour and firm texture make Honey Fungus a popular ingredient in parts of Europe, where it is sold in local markets.

It does not freeze well or reconstitute readily from the dried state, although it can be ground to produce a strongly flavoured mushroom powder that is ideal for sauces. Very small specimens may be blanched whole and then pickled in oil; these go very well with pasta dishes.

must know

Several other common fungi grow in clumps from rotting wood. The very bitter-tasting Sulphur Tuft (*Hypholoma fasciculare*), the inedible Shaggy Pholiota (*Pholiota squarrosa*) and several poisonous *Galerina* species all have a brown spore print, so make sure that your supposed Honey Fungus has white spores before you eat it.

Sulphur Tuft (*Hypholoma fasciculare*).

Jelly Tongue and Apricot Jelly

Many of the edible mushrooms described in this book can be used for making soups and other starters in addition to preparing main courses, but even the most imaginative cook will have problems coming up with a mushroom pudding! As it happens, two relatively uncommon species can be used for a dessert and both are found in coniferous woodland.

Jelly Tongue (*Pseudohydnum gelatinosum*) is an easily overlooked, grey-brown bracket-like fungus in the shape of a tongue or shoehorn that grows from conifer stumps and decaying wood. Rarely more than 7cm wide, it has a densely velvety upper surface and can be mistaken for Jew's Ear (*see* page 162). The underside of Jelly Tongue is covered with closely spaced, gelatinous white spines.

BELOW: Apricot Jelly.

BOTTOM: The underside of Jelly Tongue.

Apricot Jelly (*Guepinia helvelloides* or *Tremiscus helvelloides*) is an unusual British species that is spreading northwards. It grows from the ground or rotting wood, often among moss below conifers. It is the shape of a curled tongue or split trumpet, vivid apricot pink in colour, and it stands about 10cm high.

How to cook Jelly Tongues and Apricot Jellies

Both of these species have the texture of gelatin and can be poached in sugar or honey. With the addition of a little liqueur, they make a most unusual dessert when prepared in this way. The fungi can also be pickled and used as an addition to a main course.

Velvet Shank

Apart from Oyster Mushrooms, late-fruiting Wood Blewits and the ubiquitous Jew's Ear, there is not a lot going for the mushroom hunter in winter because of the cold temperatures. Velvet Shank (*Flammulina velutipes*), or Winter Mushroom as it is called in North America, is an exception to this – it is most plentiful in the winter, although it fruits all through the year.

The cultivation of *F. velutipes* in the dark, as pioneered by the Japanese, produces dense clusters of long, thin, white stems topped by tiny undeveloped caps. Known as Enokitake, the fungus can now be bought fresh in Britain (*see* page 63).

Velvet Shank grows as dense clusters on dead trunks, stumps and cut logs of broad-leaved trees, including Elm, Sycamore, Ash and Oak, as well as on dead Gorse stems. The flat, slimy, orange to red-brown caps grow to 8cm across. Initially white, the crowded gills mature to a yellowish brown and have a white spore print. The slender, velvety stem is pale at its apex, brown in the middle and black at the base. It lacks a ring and is often flattened and curved.

Velvet Shanks in their natural habitat.

Brown Stew Fungus.

While no other tufted fungus growing on dead wood has the dark velvety stems of Velvet Shank, one common lookalike that also fruits through the winter is the poisonous Sulphur Tuft (*see* photograph on page 158). However, its stems lack the velvet and have a ring zone, and the yellow gills become discoloured by the purple-brown spores. Sulphur Tuft also has a very bitter taste.

The edible Brown Stew Fungus (*Kuehneromyces mutabilis* or *Galerina mutabilis*) grows in clumps on stumps of broad-leaved trees. In contrast to Velvet Shank, its date-brown cap dries paler in the centre, the stem base is brown and scaly, and the gills and spore print are brown. This species must not be confused with the smaller, poisonous Funeral Bell (*Galerina marginata*; *see* page 183), it lacks the stem scales, is not tufted, has a mealy smell and is more common on coniferous wood.

How to cook Velvet Shanks

Velvet Shank is not in the top league of edible species, but its winter availability – often in large numbers – makes up for this. In addition, specimens collected in winter are only rarely maggot-infested. If you are using them fresh, first wipe away any stickiness from the caps, discard the tough stems and slice the caps.

The rather elastic consistency of Velvet Shanks requires gentle cooking, after which, like Jew's Ears, they go well with rice dishes. They can also be added to casseroles and stews. Velvet Shanks may be dried (including the stems) and ground to make mushroom powder (*see* page 58) adding this to fresh ones greatly improves the overall flavour.

Jew's Ear

For hundreds of years, prior to the days of political correctness, *Auricularia auricula-judae* was known as Jew's Ear. The suggested standardised English name is now Jelly Ear, but most mycologists are sticking with the old name, not for racist reasons (at one time all edible mushrooms were deemed 'Jew's meat') but because this fungus is part of folklore.

must know

Look for Jew's Ear on the old main stems of Elder bushes at any time of the year – it is as common in February as it is in October. The fungus is best cut from the tree with a knife, leaving the tough point of attachment behind.

The myth that Judas Iscariot hanged himself from an Elder, the principal host of Jew's Ear, is perpetuated in William Shakespeare's play *Love's Labour's Lost* (Act V, Scene II).

More than 90 per cent of the records of Jew's Ear are on Elder, although it occasionally also grows on other broad-leaved trees, including Sycamore and Beech. Initially more like inverted saucers, the gregarious fruit bodies become shell- or ear-shaped, each one measuring up to 10cm across and extending 3–4cm from its woody host. The fungus is gelatinous, rubbery and typically date-brown in colour, although much paler specimens have been recorded. It has a clammy, velvety feel, and the lower side is marked with vein-like wrinkles. In dry weather, Jew's Ears turn dark brown, shrink in size by 50 per cent, and become hard and brittle.

Jew's Ear growing on Elder.

How to cook Jew's Ears

The mild-tasting Jew's Ear is a fun fungus rather than a culinary delicacy. The worst way to prepare it is by frying it whole, as it will be very tough and is also likely to jump out of the pan, carrying hot butter or oil with it. It can be added to stir-fries, but it needs to be sliced finely first.The fungus is used more often in soups and stews, where thin slices benefit from long, slow cooking. As with its tropical relative the Wood-ear (*Auricularia cornea*), which is grown commercially (*see* page 62) and used extensively in oriental cookery, Jew's Ear is good for thickening soups and sauces. Historically, the fungus was used as a soothing medicine for eye and throat inflammation.

Jew's Ear is the easiest of all the edible fungi to dry (it may even be collected in the dry state), and is readily reconstituted by soaking in warm water for 20 minutes. Better still, grind the dried fungus to a powder and use it to add flavour to soups and sauces.

Close-up of a Jew's Ear.

There are a few species that may possibly be confused with Jew's Ear, including the Tripe Fungus (*Auricularia mesenterica*), whose undersurface is very similar but whose upper surface is tough, hairy and greyish brown. Despite its name, this fungus is inedible. The pale brown, brain-like Jelly Leaf (*Tremella foliacea*) is much softer than Jew's Ear and lacks the ear-shaped lobes.

Oyster mushrooms

Between them, the oyster mushrooms (various species of *Pleurotus*) have a long fruiting season that includes the winter, they can often be found in large numbers, and they are not easily confusable with any poisonous species.

Remember to look up when searching for oyster mushrooms, and be prepared for some climbing.

The fungi fruit on dead wood, tree trunks (of both living and dead trees), cut logs, stumps and fallen branches, most frequently on broad-leaved timber. It is worth checking both sides of any standing dead wood or old fallen tree trunks, especially where surrounding vegetation maintains moist conditions. It is also useful to make a note of the exact position of any oyster mushroom find, as each mycelium usually produces fruit for three to four years and, weather permitting, there may be two or three flushes in the same year.

Several different species of oyster mushroom (not all native to Britain) and a number of colour forms are now widely sold in shops around the country. Oyster mushrooms are among the easiest edible fungi to cultivate (*see* pages 64 and 67), and in the United States they are second only to the *Agaricus* mushrooms in terms of supermarket sales of fresh fungi. Needless to say, wild ones always seem to taste better.

Oyster Mushroom (*Pleurotus ostreatus*) is most frequent on Beech but also occurs on Poplar and even Horse-chestnut. It grows in dense overlapping clusters of up to 30 bracket-like fruits. Initially convex and with an inrolled, sinuous margin, each fan or oyster shell-shaped cap expands to reach a diameter of 20cm. The smooth cap surface varies from bluish grey to brown and often fades to creamy white with age. Its crowded white gills darken with age, produce a pale lilac spore print, and run down to the top of the very short, lateral, downy stem.

Oyster Mushroom can be found fruiting in any month of the year, but it is most frequent in the cooler months of autumn and in the run-up to Christmas. The firm, white, thick flesh smells faintly of mushrooms.

Branched Oyster Mushroom (*Pleurotus cornucopiae*) is more common from late spring to early autumn, although it, too, can be found all year round. It differs from Oyster Mushroom in its paler, creamy-beige colour and in the funnel or horn shape of each fruit body (hence its Latin specific epithet). The gills run right down to the base of the more central stem, which they cover with a raised, branching network. Many stems fuse near their bases like a candelabra. The thin, mealy-smelling flesh has an unpleasant odour in older specimens. Most records are on dead Elm, of which there has been no shortage as a result of Dutch Elm disease, itself caused by a fungus.

**Oyster Mushroom
on Beech.**

Pale Oyster Mushroom (*Pleurotus pulmonarius*) is a smaller, cream-coloured species with a white spore print. It is edible but less substantial than *P. ostreatus* and *P. cornucopiae*. Also included in the genus is Veiled Oyster Mushroom (*P. dryinus*), with a grey-white, slightly scaly, dry cap that has veil fragments at its margin. The gills do not run onto its lateral stem and they produce a white spore print. This fungus fruits singly, most frequently on Beech and Ash. It is not worth eating.

Those hunting in Scotland should look out for the edible relative of Oyster Mushroom known as Angel's Wings (*Pleurocybella porrigens*). Clusters of small (3–10cm), white, erect, fan-like fruit bodies of this species grow in moss from pieces of decaying (and often buried) coniferous wood. They are less fleshy but more tender than species of *Pleurotus*.

The only common gilled mushroom of similar size, shape, habit and habitat to the oyster mushrooms is the Olive Oysterling (*Panellus serotinus*). The shiny green-yellow cap browns with age and after frost. The gills are yellowish brown and the short lateral stalk is covered with small brown scales. This is an edible late-autumn and winter fruiting species that is

did you know?

The heartwood that provides food for *Pleurotus* species is deficient in nitrogen. The fungi supplement this deficiency by trapping nematode worms in special snare-like hyphae, making them the fungal equivalent of insectivorous plants.

Angel's Wings.

Olive Oysterling.

How to cook oyster mushrooms

All oyster mushrooms are edible, but the thick, pleasant-smelling flesh of *Pleurotus ostreatus* makes it the favourite species. In all cases, older caps are much tougher and, paradoxically, more watery, and it is even worth cutting away the stem region of young specimens as this is rubbery and more likely to contain insects or pieces of wood.

Young oyster mushrooms can be kept for four to five days in a fridge and require only a quick wipe clean before cooking. The caps can be sliced and then fried with garlic or shallots, and are best given a squeeze of lemon juice on serving to supplement their rather mild flavour. Alternatively, try stewing them in a little white wine and then thickening the sauce with cream or yogurt. Oyster mushrooms can be pickled but they are not worth freezing or drying.

most common on fallen trunks of Beech and Birch. Just below the cap skin is a gelatinous layer.

As with Oyster Mushroom, the rubbery stem of Olive Oysterling should be discarded. This fungus needs a long, slow cooking to reduce the slightly bitter flavour while at the same time keeping the flesh tender. It is a poor alternative to the true oyster mushrooms.

Beefsteak Fungus

One of the strangest species of bracket fungus is *Fistulina hepatica*, whose specific epithet relates to its liver-like appearance. In Britain, the common name for this species is Beefsteak Fungus, while the French call it *Langue de Boeuf* (meaning 'ox-tongue'). In Victorian times it was called Vegetable Beefsteak to avoid any confusion with a real piece of meat.

The intact fungus is indeed reminiscent of an ox-tongue in terms of its shape, colour and strangely roughened upper surface. When cut open, the fleshy fruit body is comparable in appearance to raw liver or streaky steak, especially as young specimens 'bleed' a red-brown juice. The paler coloured undersurface reveals tubes that, unlike those in other brackets, are easily separated from one another. There is no other British fungus like this one.

Beefsteak Fungus is most commonly found on old Oaks, growing from wounds, broken branches or stumps. It causes a brown discoloration of the heartwood, creating the highly valued

Beefsteak Fungus on oak.

so-called 'brown oak'. It is also frequent on Sweet Chestnut and, more rarely, on Beech. Search for fresh brackets between August and October, and remember to look up rather than down. 'Steaks' weighing more than a kilogram are not uncommon and they do not suffer from insect infestation.

Sliced Beefsteak
Fungus.

How to cook Beefsteak Fungus

Of all our edible fungi, this species is the one that people are most likely to disagree on – some rave about it, while others are not impressed. Age plays a part, as young specimens are not only more tender, but are less likely to have the acrid, vinegary taste of some older ones. This taste, together with the red-brown colour of the fungus, is imparted by chemicals called tannins that are extracted from the host tree. Both the texture and flavour of Beefsteak Fungus is improved by blanching or soaking in water/milk for an hour (with several liquid changes) before cooking. The fungus can be frozen raw but is at its best when eaten fresh.

Diced pieces from very young specimens may be eaten raw in salads – it goes well with pickled beetroot and many people enjoy its al dente texture. Strips can be grilled or even barbecued in the same way as steak, but really this is a fungus that benefits from long, slow cooking. It may be added to soups or stews, and is especially good when it is made into a stroganoff dish with the addition of yogurt or cream. Don't be put off when the flesh turns black during cooking.

Chicken of the Woods

Most of the bracket fungi that grow from tree trunks, stumps and dead wood are inedible. This is not down to their chemical make-up, but because their texture is either leathery or woody and thus quite indigestible. An exception to this is what used to be called Sulphur Polypore (in North America its name is Sulphur Shelf) but is now more widely known as Chicken of the Woods (*Laetiporus sulphureus*).

must know

A species that can be mistaken for Chicken of the Woods is Giant Polypore (*Meripilus giganteus*), whose very large brackets are frequently produced at the base of Beech trees or on Beech stumps. Its tougher brackets are pale brown and the white pores bruise black. It is not poisonous but is indigestible to many people. (*See* picture on page 173.)

Not only is this species relatively soft-textured, especially when young, but unlike most of the larger bracket fungi it produces new fruit bodies every year. These can be found as early as April,

Chicken of the Woods growing on Oak.

although May and June are the peak months for collection. While the brackets do remain on the host tree until the year end, their texture usually becomes dry, brittle and unappetising by late summer.

Each fan-shaped bracket can reach up to 30cm across and 5cm thick. Occasionally, only a single bracket is formed, but more often a tiered cluster of up to 20 brackets project from living or dead wood. The most common tree hosts in Britain are Oak and Sweet Chestnut, although Chicken of the Woods also grows on fruit trees such as Cherry and Pear, and on willows, False Acacia and even Yew.

The undulating bracket edge of Chicken of the Woods is initially rounded (later incurved) and feels like velvet or suede. The upper surface starts a deep orangey yellow but the pored undersurface is typically sulphur yellow. Pale yellow watery droplets are exuded from the pores of fresh specimens. With age, both top and bottom surfaces fade to a pale yellow and finally off-white.

watch out!

Some people are allergic to Chicken of the Woods – it may produce digestive upset, nausea, swollen lips or a rash. Do not collect it from Yew and make sure that it is not eaten raw. Blanch pieces before cooking and try just a small amount for the first time.

How to cook Chicken of the Woods

The firm, yellow flesh of the fungus is most tender near its outer edge, where it is also less likely to contain bark fragments. The flesh of a young bracket can be sliced thinly or cut into chunks, when it has the texture and taste of chicken breast. If the flesh is white and chalky, it is too old for culinary purposes.

Do *not* eat it raw, as it contains thermolabile toxins. Occasionally, the fungus has a sour flavour, although blanching before cooking removes this. It does not dry well (it goes very tough) but it may be frozen, especially if pre-cooked in butter. Thin strips brushed with oil can be grilled, or pieces may be added to a stir-fry. Use in place of chicken or Quorn (itself a fungus product) in a wide range of recipes. After cooking it can even be served cold in 'chicken' sandwiches.

Hen of the Woods

Hen of the Woods (*Grifola frondosa*) grows near the base of living broad-leaved trees and occasionally around their dead stumps. It is a root-rotting fungus that causes a white rot.

Look for it in September and October where there are ancient Oaks, although it very occasionally grows on other tree roots including Holly and Hazel. Unlike many bracket fungi, the fruit body of *G. frondosa* rots away within a few months, but often reappears at the same site in successive years.

The compound fruit body is about the size of a large cauliflower and takes the form of a bush-like cluster of thin, overlapping, tongue-shaped caps. These have a lobed, undulating margin and are faintly striated. The upper surface varies from grey to pale brown (usually more brown with age), while the underside is creamy-white and bears tiny pores that do not darken on handling. All the caps are united on a flattened, branched, white stem.

When young, Hen of the Woods is pliable and the caps are easily detached from the stem region. The white, fibrous flesh

did you know?

Grifola frondosa is cultivated commercially in Japan, where it is known as Maitake. It is said to contain cancer-preventing chemicals. In Victorian England, specimens collected in the wild were occasionally sold in local markets.

Hen of the Woods in its natural habitat.

should have a sweet or floury smell; older specimens are malodorous, smelling of mice or vinegar.

Mushroom hunters on the look out for Hen of the Woods or the more tender Chicken of the Woods (*see* page 170) frequently confuse both of these edible species, which are mostly found on or near Oak, with Giant Polypore (*Meripilus giganteus; see* 'must know' box *right*). When young, the fan-shaped, pale brown brackets of Giant Polypore may resemble the other two species, but the pale undersurface blackens on handling and the fungus is found mostly at the base of old Beech trees or on Beech stumps. Fully grown specimens may extend to at least a metre across, so Giant Polypore lives up to its name. When very young, the rather solid flesh of this species can be eaten, but it is not easy to digest and so is best avoided.

How to cook Hen of the Woods

Young specimens of Hen of the Woods are well worth eating, but the mild, sweet-tasting flesh needs careful preparation. First, separate the individual caps and the upper stem region (discard the tough stem base) and wipe clean. Cut larger caps into strips and stew over a low heat. Very young fungi can be blanched and then baked whole.

must know

Tree identification is very important when hunting for some of the edible bracket fungi. Hen of the Woods is largely found at the base of old Oak trees, and only rarely on Ash and Beech; Chicken of the Woods is most common on oak and Sweet Chestnut; while Giant Polypore is mostly associated with Beech.

Giant Polypore on a Beech stump.

Cauliflower Fungus

Although the Cauliflower Fungus, or Wood Cauliflower (*Sparassis crispa*), is not as common as the other edible mushrooms described in this book, a dedicated mushroom hunter should come across it in most years. Once found it is never forgotten, owing to its unusual appearance and size.

In *British Edible Fungi*, Mordecai Cooke wrote of a specimen found in Kent: 'It took two men to carry the box in which it was packed, and the box afterwards became a spacious rabbit hutch.' This was perhaps something of a fisherman's story, as *S. crispa* is normally about the size of a human head (although it does occasionally grow larger) and can weigh up to 20kg – more than enough to feed a very large family.

The first impression of the fungus is that it looks like a cross between a sponge and a cauliflower heart. Closer inspection reveals a brain-like mass of thin, folded, sinuous, flattened, leaf-like branches. On young specimens these are creamy white or pale yellow and give off a slightly sweet smell. With age, the smell becomes sharp and the fungus turns brown, starting at

must know

Look for Cauliflower Fungus in coniferous woods. It is most often found with Pine trees, either at, or within a metre of, the trunk base or, less often, on tree stumps. It may be partially hidden by a carpet of Pine needles.

Cauliflower Fungus at the base of a Pine tree.

the branch edges. A vertical cut reveals a more solid stem-like region from which the branches arise.

If your 'cauliflower' has flattened lobes and is growing with Pine, then there is no possible mistake in your identification. There is a similar species of *Sparassis* that grows with Oak or Beech, but its lobes are less sinuous and little branched. It is also rare and tough-fleshed, so should be left to grow. Some of the coral fungi are superficially similar to Cauliflower Fungus, but they are much smaller and their branches are more root-like. Very young fruit bodies of Hen of the Woods (*see* page 172) and Giant Polypore (*see* page 173) have been mistaken for *S. crispa*, but they typically grow on Oak and Beech respectively, never with Pine.

Close-up of part of a large Cauliflower Fungus.

How to cook Cauliflower Fungi

Carefully cut away the top part of the 'cauliflower', making sure that it is firm and fresh. Shake out any pine needles, dirt or insect life. In the kitchen, cut the fungus into sections to facilitate cleaning, and remove any older brown or spongy portions that could cause gastric problems. This is one of the few mushrooms that benefits from a good wash.

The nutty flavour of Cauliflower Fungus should not be masked. I prefer to fry or bake the segments in butter with the addition of parsley and a little cream or yogurt. They can also be coated in batter and then deep-fried, or added as pieces to soups and stews. Portions of young specimens can be frozen (blanch them first), pickled or dried.

Truffles

In parts of France and Italy, collecting and marketing truffles is a way of life, and they have been gathered for food for at least 4,000 years. Truffles are a group of ascomycete fungi (*see* page 33) in the genus *Tuber*, with underground fruit bodies that are prized for their aroma, flavour and supposed aphrodisiac properties.

The dark, marbled flesh of the Périgord Truffle is similar to that of the earthballs (*see* page 115), which have sometimes been substituted for the truffle.

The normally subterranean fruit of False Truffle (*Elaphomyces granulatus*), a non-edible fungus. Its position is given away by the above-ground, club-like fruit bodies of *Cordyceps ophioglossoides*, a fungal parasite that grows on it.

Underground species of the genus *Terfezia* are found and eaten in North Africa and the Middle East, and some people believe that these were the manna mentioned in the Bible. The Roman writer Pliny commented that truffles 'are distinguished by their colour, which is red, or black, or white within'.

It appears that the British were rather slow to catch on. John Gerard in his *Herball*, printed in 1597, describes and illustrates a *Cyclamen* corm under the name of *Tuber terrae*, while the first authentic British record was of *Tuber aestivum*, found at Rushton, Northamptonshire, in 1693. By this time, we were already importing truffles from France. There are more than 70 species of British fungi that produce underground fruit bodies, although many of these are no bigger than a pea and only a few are edible.

Spore dispersal of truffles is mostly effected by mammals such as squirrels, voles and pigs, which dig up and eat the fungi, distributing the spores in their faeces. Truffles have a strong scent, which enables the animals to locate them. Truffle hunters have made use of this for hundreds of years, training dogs or sows (the truffle aroma is similar to the sexual pheromones produced by boars) to sniff out the treasured finds. Truffle Flies, the larvae of which eat truffles, are also attracted by the smell, and their hovering swarms can be used to locate the fungi growing below.

Sadly, the Périgord Truffle, or Black Truffle (*Tuber melanosporum*), is not found in Britain, nor is the Piedmont Truffle, or White Truffle (*Tuber magnatum*), which is mostly collected in Italy. The latter regularly commands prices in excess of £1,500 a kilogram. The species that does grow in Britain is the Summer Truffle (*Tuber aestivum*). It was collected from Wiltshire, Buckinghamshire, Sussex and Kent until the 1930s. They are still gathered in parts of France and Italy, but retail at a mere £50 a kilogram.

Summer Truffle is most likely to occur in chalky soil under Beech trees (truffles are mycorrhizal) in southern England, but without a trained dog or pig you are likely to walk over them. The only one I have seen in more than 30 years of searching had just broken through the soil surface.

The hard, subterranean Summer Truffle is roughly spherical and up to 7cm in diameter. The outer surface is covered in dark brown-black pyramidal warts, giving it the look of a rounded pine cone. Inside, the pale brown flesh is marbled with white veins. Unlike the Périgord Truffle, which has a dark brown marbled flesh and a very rich aroma, Summer Truffle has a less distinctive smell.

ABOVE: A French truffle hunter with his pig.

LEFT: Summer Truffle just showing above the ground.

must know

A smooth-skinned, red-brown edible species of fungus, formerly known as the Red Truffle of Bath (*Melanogaster variegatus*), is in fact a subterranean puffball.

How to cook Summer Truffles

Carefully brush or wash soil away from the warty skin and then use shavings of the raw fungus to add flavour to pâtés, stuffings, scrambled eggs, omelettes and other egg dishes. You can also steep a few shavings in olive oil to make aromatic truffle oil, which can be used sparingly in dressings or drizzled over savoury dishes – a little goes a long way. Truffles will keep in a refrigerator for up to a week, but keep them well wrapped or everything else will become infused with their taste.

5 Poisonous Species

The fear of being poisoned is the main reason why most British people don't indulge in mushroom hunting. Our culture is one that depicts the majority of fungi as toadstools and all toadstools as deadly poisonous. In fact, there are relatively few poisonous species. This chapter will help you to familiarise yourself with them.

Poisonous species

More than 100 edible species are collected and then eaten, and most other fungi are merely inedible rather than actually poisonous to humans.

There are only about 20 common poisonous lookalikes (species that could be confused with collectable edible species), of which a third are potentially lethal, if eaten. There is a deeply ingrained belief (still promulgated by a few modern writers) that even touching a poisonous species will result in dire consequences. In fact, less than 5 per cent of British fungi with fruit bodies large enough to be of culinary interest are poisonous.

Of the thousands of calls made annually to poisons information centres, very few concern mushrooms and half of those that do, involve small children. There have been no recent British fatalities from accidental fungal poisoning. Despite this, any mushroom hunter with a future must always identify

must know

Being able to give an accurate description of what has been consumed in the event of a suspected poisoning is important. Better still, keep aside a few fruit bodies from each collection in the fridge; when all is well, they can be consumed at a second sitting.

Some poisonous species like The Sickener (*Russula emetica*) are not easily confused with any edible species.

collected edible species carefully and be able to recognise their poisonous lookalikes. In short, there is a need to know both friends and enemies.

Several of our most poisonous species, including two look-alikes, are in the genus *Amanita*. They fruit from summer to late autumn and are associated with trees in woods, gardens and parks. There are over 30 *Amanita* species in Britain though not all are poisonous. A young *Amanita* fruit body is enclosed in an egg-like universal veil. After pushing through this the cap may be speckled with veil remnants. A sac-like volva encircles the stem base. The creamy-white crowded gills are free of the stem and deposit a white spore print.

Death Cap (*Amanita phalloides*) has a smooth, sweet-smelling, olive-green or bronze-coloured cap that is usually devoid of veil remnants. It is commonest in Beech and Oak woods of southern England. The rarer **Destroying Angel** (*Amanita virosa*) is completely white with a deeply domed cap. It frequents mixed broad-leaved woodland. Both Death Cap and Destroying Angel superficially resemble *Agaricus* mushrooms.

Death Cap, showing the volva, ring and olive-green cap.

Initial symptoms following ingestion of Death Cap or Destroying Angel include severe stomach ache, profuse sweating, nausea, diarrhoea and a fall in blood pressure. Later other poisons including amanita toxins destroy cells in the liver and kidneys, often with fatal consequences.

Panther Cap (*Amanita pantherina*) has an eggcup-like volva and a brown cap with white spots. It is an occasional species of Beech and Oak woods and contains toxins similar to those found in the red and white spotted **Fly Agaric** (*Amanita muscaria; see* picture on page 74). Despite reports to the contrary neither species is lethal but they can produce alarming symptoms mostly due to their influence on the nervous system.

Destroying Angel.

Panther Cap.

The Blusher (*Amanita rubescens*) is a very common species occurring in a wide range of woodlands. It has a pale brownish-buff cap, a bulbous base to its stem and an indistinct volva. Where the cap and stem flesh is exposed to air it turns pink. Some books (*see* page 54) insist that this is a safe *Amanita* but it contains chemicals that destroy red blood cells. Although these chemicals are detoxified by the heat of cooking it is not worth taking a chance with this fungus.

Similar dangerous toxins to those found in Death Cap and Destroying Angel are also found in the aptly named **Funeral Bell** (*Galerina marginata*) which is most frequently found growing on the dead branches of coniferous trees. Despite its smaller size (caps to 6 cm across), mealy smell and red-brown spore print it has been mistaken for Honey Fungus (*see* page 156). Although often occurring in large numbers Funeral Bell does not grow in tufts and lacks the dark stem base of the edible Velvet Shank (*see* page 160).

Potentially fatal kidney damage may also result through the consumption of some species of *Cortinarius* found growing on the ground in woods. The protective veil covering the young gills of these fungi looks like a spider's web, their stems lack a true ring and the spore print is rusty brown. Of the hundreds of species in Britain, some have lilac gills and resemble the pink-spored Wood Blewit (*see* page 97). **Cortinarius orellanus** and related orange-brown species smelling of radishes have been mistaken for Chanterelles (*see* page 130), despite differences in smell, gill attachment and spore colour.

Cortinarius alboviolaceus.

Red-staining Inocybe, showing red on the cap, gills and stem.

The dangers of eating **False Morel** (*Gyromitra esculenta*) are outlined in the 'Must know' box on page 129. As with some species of *Amanita* and *Cortinarius*, this fungus contains chemicals capable of causing fatal liver damage. Unfortunately, its fruiting season overlaps with that of the morels.

The toxin muscarine also occurs in two small, lilac-coloured woodland fungi that resemble Amethyst Deceiver (*see* page 149). The more potent of these is **Lilac Inocybe** (*Inocybe geophylla* var. *lilacina*), with brown gills and spores, and a raised centre to its cap. The less poisonous **Lilac Bell Cap** (*Mycena pura*) smells of radishes and has pinkish-grey gills. The **Red-staining Inocybe** (*Inocybe patouillardii*) is larger than

Devil's Bolete.

the Lilac Inocybe, but it also has brown spores and a raised cap centre with brick-red fibres, and it bruises the same colour. It has been mistaken for the Field Mushroom and St George's Mushroom, but is largely confined to woodland clearings and parkland, especially in combination with Beech on chalk soil.

In addition to Cep and the other edible boletes (*see* pages 116–125), the *Boletus* genus contains some poisonous species, including the common **Boletus luridus** and **Boletus erythropus**, both with orange-red pores. In parts of Europe these are eaten after careful preparation, but this is not recommended, especially as *B. luridus* reacts with alcohol and both species can be confused with **Devil's Bolete** (*B. satanus*). The latter is a rare species, with a raised red network on its stem in addition to orange-red pores. It is not quite as deadly as its name implies, but it does cause nausea, sweating and heart palpitations if consumed.

Some collectors consider that eating grassland fungi is much safer than risking the poisonous lookalikes of many woodland edibles. This is a risky assumption to make, however, as there are dangerous grassland lookalikes that must be recognised even by those who limit themselves to collecting Field Mushrooms. **Yellow-staining Mushroom** (*Agaricus xanthoderma*) is one such species, and is easily mistaken for Field or Wood mushrooms – *see* page 86. It grows in grassland but is also found in gardens and in woodland leaf litter. Its greyish-pink gills have a sharp smell like urine or ink, and the cut stem base and bruised cap turn chrome-yellow. Most people are not affected by Yellow-staining Mushroom, but others suffer sickness and diarrhoea for about two days after eating it.

The edible Fairy Ring Champignon (*see* page 104) can be gathered in large numbers but is easily confused with a very poisonous grassland lookalike. **Sweating Mushroom**, also known as **Fool's Funnel** (*Clitocybe rivulosa* or *C. dealbata*), grows in rings and contains large amounts of muscarine, the poison found in Panther Cap and Fly Agaric. Sweating Mushroom fruits from midsummer to late autumn. Its cap is creamy white, often with patches of pink or pale brown, and measures up to 4cm across. The cap soon flattens, is often depressed in the centre and has an inrolled margin. Some specimens exhibit concentric fissures near the cap margin. The crowded, decurrent creamy-grey gills leave a white spore print. The flesh smells of meal or sperm, and the tough stalk is non-pliable.

A number of small grassland fungi with pink spores are poisonous. **The Livid Pinkgill** (*Entoloma sinuatum*) sometimes grows at field edges and has been mistaken for Field Mushroom and The Miller (*see* pages 85 and 146), although it is less frequent and larger than both of these species. Equally, some brown- and black-spored little brown fungi contain toxins, including the **Magic Mushroom** (*see* page 70). To avoid confusion with any of these lookalikes when collecting Fairy Ring Champignons, check that your specimens produce a white spore print.

Glossary

adnate Broadly attached to the stem (referring to gills or tubes).

adnexed Narrowly attached to the stem (referring to gills or tubes).

agaric A soft-bodied fungus with a stem and umbrella-shaped cap.

Ascomycetes A group of fungi that produce spores in an ascus.

ascus An elongated hyphal segment, usually containing eight spores.

Basidiomycetes A group of fungi that produce spores on a basidium.

basidium A club-shaped hyphal segment, usually bearing four spores.

blanch To immerse briefly in boiling water and then in ice-cold water.

bolete An agaric with tubes (not gills) that can be detached from the cap.

bracket fungus A species that grows shelf-like, usually pored, fruit bodies on wood.

bulbous Swollen like a bulb (referring to a stem base).

cap The part of the fruit body that carries the spore-bearing tissue.

conifer A tree that produces seeds in cones, including pines and larches.

convex Curved like the exterior of a sphere (referring to the cap).

cortina A cobweb-like veil that protects the immature gills of some agarics.

deliquescent Dissolving into a liquid (referring to the cap and gills).

distant Well spaced (referring to the gills).

excentric (eccentric) Not centred, but attached to one side.

family A group of closely related genera.

flesh The interior tissue of the stem and of the cap above the gills or pores.

free Not connected to the stem (referring to gills or tubes).

fruit body The reproductive organ of a fungus.

genus (pl. **genera**) A group of closely related species.

gill The blade-like, vertical, spore-bearing tissue found on the undersurface of most agaric caps.

glutinous Made sticky by a glue-like deposit (referring to the cap or stem).

habit The mode of growth, e.g. singly, in rings, tufted.

habitat Where an organism lives, e.g. on grazed grassland, in oak woodland.

hallucinogen A drug that alters perception.

hypha (pl. **hyphae**) A filamentous branching tube.

mealy With the odour or taste of dough or damp flour.

mushroom An edible fungus; a species of *Agaricus*; or any gill-bearing agaric.

mycelium (pl. **mycelia**) A mass of hyphae; the vegetative part of a fungus.

mycorrhiza A beneficial relationship between a fungus and the roots of a plant (especially tree roots).

parasite An organism that lives at the expense of another (called the host).

polypore A fungus with a hard or tough fruit body that produces spores in tubes (cf. bracket fungus).

pore The open end of a tube in polypores and boletes.

rhizomorph A mass of hyphae, forming the root-like 'bootlaces' in Honey Fungus.

ring The collar-like remnants of a partial veil found on the stem of some agarics.

saprophyte An organism that lives off dead or decaying matter.

sinuate Notched near the point of attachment to the stem (referring to gills).

species A group of organisms capable of interbreeding with one another.

spore The typically unicellular reproductive unit of a fungus.

spore print The pattern produced by the release of spores from a fruit body.

stem/stalk/stipe The usually cylindrical part of a fruit body that supports the cap and links it with the substrate.

substrate The surface on which a fruit body grows, e.g. soil, wood, dung.

thermolabile A substance that breaks down when heated. This applies to the toxins in some fungi, which are destroyed when the fungi are cooked; these species must not be eaten raw.

toadstool A poisonous fungus; any gill-bearing agaric.

transient Not present for very long (referring to a feature such as a ring).

truffle A highly prized edible fungus; an ascomycete fungus species with subterranean fruit bodies, some of which are edible.

tube A narrow, cylindical spore-bearing structure that replaces a gill in boletes and polypores.

veil A protective covering enclosing a fruit body. A partial veil covers only the young gills or tubes, while a universal veil encloses the entire immature fruit body.

volva The cup- or sac-like remnants of the universal veil surrounding the stem base of some fungi.

Need to know more?

The British Mycological Society
Joseph Banks Building
Royal Botanic Gardens
Kew
Richmond
London TW9 3AB
www.britmycolsoc.org

Maintains a fungal records database and organises forays and workshops for keen amateurs. The society also publishes and academic journal, *The Mycologist*. A separate subscription can be taken for *Field Mycology*, an excellent quarterly magazine for the study and identification of wild fungi, which is aimed at the interested amateur.

British Wildlife magazine
British Wildlife Publishing
The Old Dairy
Milton on Stour
Gillingham
Dorset SP8 5PX
Tel: 01747 835511
www.britishwildlife.com

Includes in-depth articles on fungi, reports on interesting finds and excellent book reviews.

Plantlife
Plantlife International
14 Rollestone Street
Salisbury SP1 1DX
Tel: 01722 342730
www.plantlife.org.uk

A charity which is actively involved in the conservation of some of our rarer mushrooms and toadstools, and has carried out fungal surveys with the help of it members.

Books

Benjamin, Denis, *Mushrooms: Poisons and Panaceas* (New York: W. H. Freeman and Company, 1995).

Courtecuisse, Regis, *Mushrooms of Britain and Europe* (Collins Wildlife Trust Guide, London: HarperCollins, 1999).

Harding, Patrick, *Mushrooms*, 2nd edn (Collins Gem Guide, London: HarperCollins, 2003).

Jordan, Peter and Wheeler, Steven, *The Practical Mushroom Encyclopedia* (London: Anness Publishing, 2004).

Mabey, Richard, *Food for Free* (London: HarperCollins, 2001).

Matossian, Mary, *Poisons of the Past:*
Molds, Epidemics and History (New
Haven, CT, and London: Yale University
Press, 1989).

Oldridge, S., Pegler, D. and Spooner, B.,
Wild Mushroom and Toadstool Poisoning
(Kew: Royal Botanic Gardens, 1989).

O'Reilly, Pat, *Multimedia Guide to Fungi*,
CD-ROM (Llandysul: First Nature,
2005).

Pegler, David, *Kingfisher Field Guide to the*
Mushrooms and Toadstools of Britain and
Europe (London,Kingfisher, 1990).

Philips, Roger, *Mushrooms and Others*
Fungi of Great Britain and Europe
(London: Pan Books, 1981).

Spooner, Brian, and Roberts, Peter, *Fungi*
(Collins New Naturalist 96, London:
HarperCollins, 2005).

Watling, Roy, *Fungi* (London: Natural
History Museum, 2003).

Index